The
Dating Story

An Encoded Guide to Dating, Engagement, and Marriage

J. D. Baker

The Dating Story

A Policy Found in an Old Story

Published by 21st Century Press Springfield, MO 65807

21st Century Press is a Christian publisher dedicated to publishing books that have a high standard of family values. We believe the vision for our books is to provide families and individuals with user-friendly materials that will help them in their daily lives and experiences. It is our prayer that this book will help you discover Biblical truth for your own life and help you meet the needs of others. May God richly bless you.

21st Century Press
2131 W. Republic Rd.
PMB 211
Springfield, MO 65807
email: lee@21stcenturypress.com

Cover and Book Design: Lee Fredrickson
ISBN: TP 978-1-951774-08-0
ISBN: Ebook978-1-951774-09-7
Visit our website at: www.21stcenturypress.com
Printed in the United States of America

21stCENTUR
P   R   E   S
READING YOU LOUD AND CLE

DEDICATION

There are very few people in the world, like Rebekah in this story. But I am married to one.

This book would still be unreadable and in a rough draft if not for my wife Connie, who would consider watering ten camels a necessity, no matter how hard. If not for her and the encouragement from friends, my notes would still be my notes.

CONTENTS

FOREWORD

Tell me a story, especially one I can relate to. Stories captivate us, move us, teach us, better us. Avoid the boring; instead tell a story and apply it well. This is precisely what Jim Baker has done. He has taken the 4000-year-old story of finding Rebekah for Isaac, and has turned it into a helpful guide for today.

Three millennia ago, Solomon was enthralled with "the way of a man with a maid" (Proverbs 30:18-19). The world still gawks, with mouths wide open, at the beautiful wonder of a love story. We never cease to marvel at how two lives can become knit, and so intertwined that they become one.

Jim's method in approaching this phenomenon is simple. He tells the story piece by piece, verse by verse. At every pivotal moment, he takes time to share how this successful bonding can be redone today.

Things have not changed much in the "guy meets girl; girl likes guy" world. The progressive steps are the same: focus, tease, finesse, assess, grow serious, and then enjoy that magical bonding.

Along the path of this beautiful process are many places where two "lovebirds" can stumble and fall. Jim's book shines here. He helps us see in advance where the pitfalls might be, where we might stub our toe.

On the romance journey, it helps to have someone walking close beside us, giving us wise counsel. Jim does this for his readers. Let him help you. Walk the relationship road with him. This book will help you enjoy the stroll.

–Dr. John Marshall

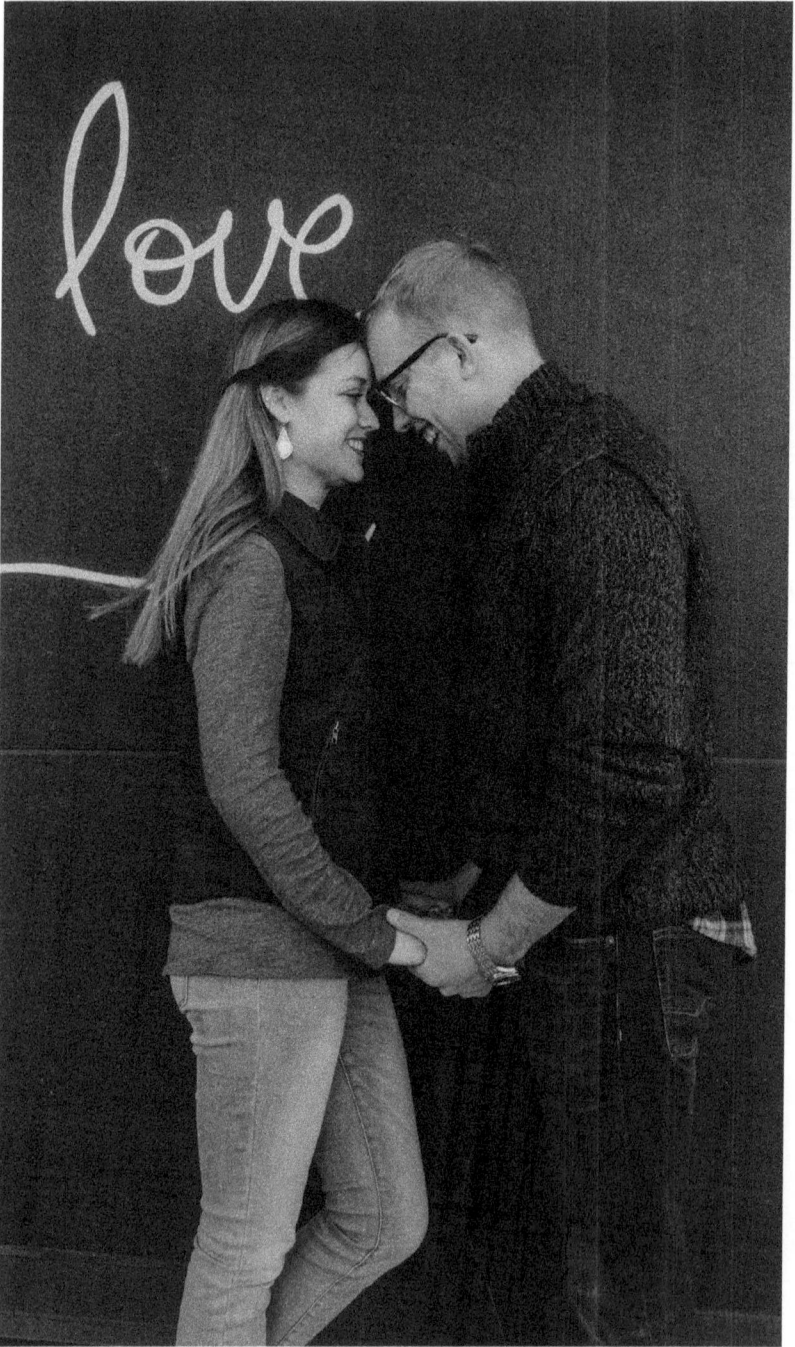

PREFACE

THE NEW NORMAL — DATING

Think of this book as an investigation into the way families form and function today. I believe the "family unit" has changed, but not everybody would agree. Why not? Because as culture evolves, we often don't see it happen and there is no reason to question what we have.

It is difficult to know when normal things around us change. For example, before the introduction of the iPhone, nobody would consider carrying a computer in their pocket as normal behavior. But there are a growing number of people who have never known life without a smartphone. We seldom consider the past and how things have evolved.

History has something to tell us that is significant about one of the most "normal" things we hold dear - family. Our question to consider is, "Has family-life always been the way we know it today?

What if we discover that there has been a transformation in the way family is formed that affected the way it functions? Understanding this might allow us to evaluate the difference and ask the question, "Is the new normal better?"

It is not my purpose in this book to analyze the modern family – the good or the bad. We all can do this on our own. I hear a lot of conversation and concern for families and how they are functioning. It seems something is different - what happened?

It is part of history. One of the critical steps of forming a family has radically changed, and nobody seems to have noticed. Everybody saw it happen, but I'm not sure anybody understood what was taking place. The change started about a hundred years ago, way before my time. I had no clue what was going on years later as a teenager.

The New Norm - Dating

The unseen change started with the introduction of a new concept called "dating." Dating now has become the cultural way —a family norm. It is often just an accidental meeting that slowly evolves into a family. Our current culture has never known anything else.

But, from what I see and hear, there is nothing easy about dating today. There is not much of a guarantee with dating or marriage that a person will not end up alone with battle scars. Something has changed, and marital relationships are different - and not necessarily for the better. It all began with a change in how people meet and form a marriage. It all evolved from there.

After we see what has taken place, we will look back into ancient history and find specific methods to do "dating" THAT WILL give assurance in a marital relationship. These are not my ideas. I found them in a quaint Bible story written almost 4000 years old. Unknowingly, I used this "dating tactic" some 50 years ago. But it took a conversation years later for me to understand the value of this narrative. Here is how my study started.

An older man I respected, said something I never anticipated him to say. He was not a hard-headed Bible thumper, but he was rock solid and always had been a man of high integrity. The topic he brought up was not a surprise, but the implication that he approved was more than my face could conceal.

He appeared happy about a family member who moved in with his girlfriend. The very thing he "viciously condemned" his whole life had somehow become "acceptable." My question was simple, "What caused the shift in what he once proclaimed so loudly as wrong?" What happened?

What changed our culture?

It was not hard to figure out, but I fear doing things God's way is almost lost. How could those who preached God's truth have forgotten what they once believed? Maybe God was wrong, and our culture has found a better way?

Think about it. Think about it some more – NO WAY! God is not wrong.

If you don't understand that something is different, look around, watch the News, read the tweets, and listen to people talk. You do not have to look very far to see the relationship we call marriage is not working very well. Family life is nothing like it used to be.

In the new normal, we seldom see anything about God's plan. He was the one who created the institution of marriage. His concept and process of marriage can be found in the Bible, and His ways HAVE produced enduring marriages and families. This old story is full of hints on how to do modern dating the right way—God's way.

If you think God is too busy to help you write your life or romance story, you're wrong. He has already set everything in place. Are you paying attention to what God is doing in your life?

So, a little tiny thought entered my mind. Take the years of notes I have on the topic and write a book; after all, I watched the change take place.

But I felt that nobody would want to read such a book. Then a still small voice said, "What if one person would read the book and see how biblical marriage works? Would you write a book for one person?"

The answer was yes.

Perhaps, it is written for you.

INTRODUCTION

The Dating Story

As Found in an "Old" Manuscript Genesis 24
Proving All Things for Marriage

Let's start by looking at a clever deception that has taken place. One of the results of this may be our culture's current marriage nightmare. If you haven't noticed, marriage is not working very well for some in our society. And I suspect it all started with dating. We need to look at how this deception has tried to change God's concept of dating and marriage. Marriage is quickly becoming meaningless in our culture – it's just a legal snare to some. And the falsehood has grown large with the biblical view becoming almost non-existent. I make this statement because of the reactions received when others hear how long I have been married to my first and only wife, as if it is not possible for a marriage to last that long. Many cannot relate to this at all, thinking it impossible. Their implied question is, "Why would you want to be married to one person that long?"

Ouch, the last point is the latest game changer in the deception. I just think of it as "The Lie." These kinds of thoughts are the result of a century-long war on relationships. Nevertheless, a lasting marriage is possible, and there are innumerable reasons you would say, "I want to be married," and fifty years later say, "I still want to be married." It all makes sense if you know the secret to God's design for marriage.

Marriage is defined and illustrated in the Bible, but not just in one place. Nevertheless, all we need to know is still in plain sight. It has been hidden from our understanding because of cultural changes. It seems the movers and shakers of our society don't always want marriage.

The Bible holds secrets and tactics on how we can do marriage right, and it starts with dating. It is all in a charming Bible story on marriage. As we move through the story, look for subtle ways the Bible points these things out. As they become clear, it is obvious we are to apply them to our lives.

Think of this as an adventure.

It is a quest for romance, and like buried treasure, it must be found by searching and digging. Part of the adventure will be finding a missing word we hear so often in our culture. This word is in the story but not where you would expect it to be. I am not going to tell you the word, but you will understand "why" when you discover it. It's part of the "romance."

Who should read this book? In my opinion, it would be beneficial to those about to begin dating, parents, or anyone with a marriage in trouble or suffering from the tragedy of divorce.

The critical need for this truth is for those about to start the adventure of dating. Unfortunately, as we will see, the secret for success is almost lost with few knowing why.

This old Bible story will show the way.

Parents would be the next in line to benefit. As they see the truth unfold and share the ways of successful dating with their children, future heartaches may be avoided.

Those with divorce either behind them or before them can find hope for the future in Genesis 24 - this story still applies. Be astonished and recognize what God can do.

What is the expected result of this book? Marriage filled with a lifetime of romance.

Some backstage information is needed to set up this ancient

narrative and help us understand current dating practices. This new dating concept started slowly then exploded and became part of Baby Boomer history. We all need to know what occurred so we can utilize this incredible biblical account about courtship and how to do dating right.

One

THE GENERATIONAL DIVIDE

The big "divide" exploded in the nineteen-sixties, but Satan started this attack on marriage about one hundred years ago. Three wars provide the framework that brought about what Satan wanted. Give the evil one a little crack to work his deceptions, and he will take full advantage of it.

There was not much Satan could do to infiltrate a Bible-believing and obedient family, but he saw his chance with World War One. There was a slight change in how single men and women met at this point in history. Then, during World War Two, as our nation got involved in a monster war, women had to join the workforce in large numbers.

Dating, for the first time, was introduced into our history on a large scale. The family's influence on whom a person married took a back seat - if it had any influence at all on the marriage process. Marriage without family involvement started to be driven only by physical considerations. Nevertheless, it was the Vietnam War that brought the last and most significant change. World War II was a big failure for Satan. His attack on the Jewish people was a continuation of his attack on the Seed he started back in the Old Testament as seen in Genesis 3:15. Satan knew that the Messiah was coming from Abraham, and he has been on the attack ever since.

He lost big time with the death of Hitler. Nevertheless, he used his failure in the war to produce a significant rift among the generations. I doubt he had it planned; he is just good at making little cracks into big canyons. It is an intriguing story, but don't expect to hear about it on television or social media. Here is how it went down.

The men who fought WWII became known as the Greatest Generation. They defeated Hitler, who was trying to kill off all the Jews. Israel was chosen by God to take His Hope to all the world. While the people of Israel never did much on their own, Jesus came to earth through this family. And Hitler hated them. WWII was a Religious war. Our troops that fought this battle were men who prayed their way through it. Note, WWII was not just about oil, as some historians tell the story. Oil was part of it, but the evil desire of Satan was to kill the Jews. Hitler was his tool. His evil was working overtime in the background.

Hitler believed in a "supreme race" – his choice, of course, was the Germans. To him, men were not created equal. Hitler oppressed everybody, but the Jews seemed to be his favorite target. His goal was to execute them all, partly because they were God's people, and partially because God's people would speak out about what he was doing. They would expose him. They were in his way. So, he set out to kill them off.

The Greatest Generation defeated Hitler and came home victorious. It was only after the war that the world found out the full truth about the concentration camps and mass murders carried out by Hitler. The oppression of innocent people was beyond comprehension. The Greatest Generation had selflessly stopped one of the worst evils the world had ever seen. They may not have realized the ugliness of the terror they were fighting, but they knew enough. They were heroes, and rightfully so.

The soldiers returned home as champions, but heroes shouldn't free one oppressed people group and at the same time oppress another. But that is what happened. The question was, did this Great Generation believe in real equality for all men or not? Time would eventually expose the oppression that we as a nation had ignored for generations.

Jump forward to my generation called the Baby Boomers.

Boomers were the first generation to grow up with the invention of television, more specifically the Evening News. Boomers became defined by rebellion in general. It all started with racism in the south hitting the airwaves. Television changed everything. The entire country could see what was happening anywhere, at any time. And with selective editing, a TV News Department could make sizzling hot news out of anything. For example:

> "You can't drink from this water fountain because of skin color."

It seems, in everyday life this kind of thing was ignored – but enforced. The Evening News was showing what was going on. What the Boomers saw was oppression. The News Media was young, but it already was working the Christian-based-culture in our country to expose and create dramatic News. What would Jesus say about this kind of injustice? This could not be ignored. How was this different than Hitler's actions? Hitler started with small oppressive ideas, and we know the result.

If Boomers turned to their war heroes for help, they found hypocrisy. Some of the war heroes were ignoring this oppression of color. They died to free the Jews but were openly oppressing some of their own countrymen because of skin color. When thinking about this, one would conclude this can't be true! But it was. Our heroes did not step up to the plate and fix this harassment. Their silence was the same as approval. And it seems, there was no intention of changing it.

This lack of concern for all men being equal energized the Boomers' ingrained Christian principles. These principles were deeply rooted in us by this Great Generation. As Boomers opposed the hypocrisy of their government, there was a side effect nobody saw coming. I'm talking about the Church. While churches may not have approved, their almost total silence became the same as approval. When you know something is wrong and keep quiet – that's approval. Want proof? Totally "black" or totally "white" Churches were the norm. What Would Jesus Do?

The Boomers proceeded to reject this hypocrisy and challenged the government for ignoring God's truths and basic human rights. They used the news-hungry media to preach their message. People who agree with Jesus should not discriminate because of skin color. Everybody is equal in God's eyes. The government was not responding and had to be forced to correct the issues. It was a long process, and this generational rebellion against injustice and hypocrisy resulted in the Boomers not trusting their parents, their parents' government or their parents' organized Church.

The ultimate casualty was marriage.

The Boomers maintained some level of respect for their elders and the church; they just rejected many of their beliefs. You can see in the songs of the Sixties the hatred for governmental policies. And with the Vietnam War, emotions moved to an almost explosive level. Songs like, "If I had a Hammer," "Blowing in the Wind," plus so many others tell the story. The Boomers somehow knew they could not change their parents or the Church, but they could attempt to change government policies. And the television gave the Boomers considerable political power in which to do it.

Behind the scenes, the Boomers, through stubborn determination to right a wrong, unknowingly redefined marriage. They came to view marriage as a "church thing" and unnecessary. They used the hypocrisy they had seen and cried out to change the attitude of willful oppression. Their target was man made laws. The silence of the church resulted in God's laws being thrown out like the baby with the bath water. Boomers, empowered by the emerging media, got to the place they could do whatever they wanted to do. Who could stop them? They spread their "Free Love" and "Peace" social movement around the world.

Empowered by the development and availability of birth control pills in the mid-sixties, everything changed. Here is what Wikipedia has to say about the resulting sexual revolution:

> Sexual liberation included increased acceptance of sex outside of traditional heterosexual monogamous relationships. The normalization of contraception and the pill, public nudity, pornography, premarital sex, homosexuality, and alternative forms of sexuality, and the legalization of abortion all followed.

This all happened from the time I entered High School until graduation from the State University. In less than ten years, many major social values changed. My guess is this change is not reversible. Satan and his World System had pulled off a most significant takeover, and nobody saw it coming.

I wasn't part of this movement and did not agree with the extremes. From my pre-teen years, my focus was set on God's ways. Hypocrisy was all around, and I saw how truth was rejected. But I could not "throw out" God's truth. The social movement's philosophy was clear, "If the Church was wrong on one thing, it was probably wrong on other things, maybe everything." In the total rejection of God's definition and plan, marriage became optional. Birth control created a new spirit of freedom. And this non-commit sexual revolution rapidly diminished the family connection. Do-what-you-want-to-do was the word on the street. The family became an additional casualty of the hypocrisy of the Greatest Generation and rejection of God's plan of marriage by the Boomer Generation. With easy access to birth control pills, sexual activity moved outside of marriage. It had free reign and was everywhere. Sexual glitz can turn the head of anybody. The "practical" need to raise a family with two parents was no longer a social necessity. The government began to create programs to help those who had no family support – and there were millions of children in need. This incomplete family unit became politically valuable to those elected to office. Taking care of those in need created a voter base that was not influenced by the truth. You don't vote out those who are feeding you.

So, oppression was back. Elected officials used their "captive" voter base to stay in power. It may not have been intended at first, but with no way out of poverty, those trapped in the system would have to keep their politically based checks coming. It was a "win-win" for the politicians and a "lose-lose" situation of oppression for those trapped. First, we had racial discrimination, then political oppression – both are wrong.

Since marriage was not necessary, the family had to exist with the result. The Baby Boomers' definition of marriage destroyed the concept of faithfulness. Trust in marriage was gone. Families no longer had the "glue" needed to hold them together. The result was a high divorce rate and the most prominent losers, the children.

Without a cohesive family, children now faced a life of suffering from extreme emotional and physical needs not being met. The security of the family was broken. Many children believed they somehow "caused" the separation and divorce. The stabilizing power of "marriage" to keep families together was gone. The list of casualties goes beyond the marriage to include the children.

I want to be careful here. Divorce is a fact of life. I'm not judgmental. There is enough pain in a divorce without oppression from outsiders. It is not what God planned. God hates divorce. A rampant divorce rate is a result of rejecting God's plan for marriage and family. You may not be able to go back and fix a divorce, but if you are starting over you can implement a few simple biblical principles and not go through it again.

"Cleaving" is the spiritual component of marriage, and when it is left out, problems result. Cleaving means being glued together as soul-mates. To cleave was God's part of marriage. God's glue produced a relationship that needed nobody else, physically, emotionally and spiritually. God's plan had three parts of glue. In the Baby Boomer's "loose" new definition of relationships between men and women, trust and faithfulness were lost. Because of the Sixties Social Revolution, Satan and his World System won.

I should note, it is common that both parents in a divorce pour their lives into their children without believing in a biblical marriage. The things built into our DNA cannot be changed by Satan. The Baby Boomers loved their children, but many rejected their parents' belief in biblical marriage and their parents' Churches. The foundation they were raised on was no longer trusted. The resulting alternate "marriage-like" arrangements have not worked out very well for families.

Did you notice the word "trust" entered the conversation? Trust is foundational to the concept of oneness. The Father, Son, and Holy Spirit have complete unity because they all agree on the truth. Remember part of the definition of marriage is "be one." To "be one" is more than a physical thing. It also requires the oneness of the soul, which is where we get the term soul-mate. Unity is with each other and God. When the spiritual connection is in place, then you have a relationship that pulls you together in trust.

Anytime you leave out God's ways, it results in evil. Remember, God created us all equal, but hypocrisy fueled racism, and that fight is not over. Satan loves confusion; it works well for him, especially in marriage.

The history I just presented exposes the monumental problem we all face - oppression. Many of the problems experienced today in dating and marriage are connected to this history. It is always the same problem. God's ways are rejected and replaced with private agendas.

As this book is being written, the News is full of accusations of sexual abuse and court cases coming from everywhere. These situations reek of oppression and have ruined lives. Single parents are struggling to feed and raise children. The task of one person doing the work of two is also oppressive. And the political solution ends up being nothing much more than a way to stay in power.

So, there you have it. The Greatest Generation started the dominos falling. When the Boomers rejected their parents' morals, their faith in God began to diminish, and the consequence has produced a lot of difficulties that God never intended for His Creation to have.

All future Generations now must deal with this mess. Some are turning back to the core family concept, trying to make it work. Those who are born-again and clinging to God's Word can do well even with the culture in which they were born.

This quick look backstage has shown that the story of marriage is part of the monumental battle for God's Kingdom. Marriage is beautiful, but Satan has been attacking since the beginning. We need to know our enemy and recognize his tactics. Otherwise "The Lie" will never let you experience what God has designed for you.

We have seen what happened to marriage in the sixties, and I think we can agree, this "new way" doesn't work very well. The result has created a mega-mess over the many years that followed.

So, what's the point? Oneness.

God is the ultimate example. His creation of man was to have that same perfect unity as He has. But the day Adam and Eve took the forbidden fruit, this oneness died with their spirit.

Two

What's Wrong With Marriage?

The word "dating" is not in the Bible. Nor is the concept of dating. But the process is found in an old Bible story. A story that tells us all we need to know to stay married.

I love music. Music tells the stories we love to hear. And songs have been an essential part of God's creation. Look at David's Psalms; they are dominant in his story. And everyone knows that songs of the sixties ruled. For us Baby Boomers the "songs" tell our story. It's not a complicated tale. In fact, one old Rock and Roll song will explain it all. It is by a group called Three Dog Night. A single song that puts into perspective the explosive decade of the sixties. Ten short years that changed the world forever.

> One is the loneliest number that you'll ever do
> Two can be as bad as one
> It's the loneliest number since the number one
> No is the saddest experience you'll ever know
> Yes, it's the saddest experience you'll ever know
> 'Cause one is the loneliest number that you'll ever do
> One is the loneliest number, whoa-oh, worse than two
> It's just no good anymore since you went away
> Now I spend my time just making rhymes of yesterday
> One is the loneliest number
> One is the loneliest number

The song goes on from here and keeps repeating the same words over and over. You can't miss what it is saying: One is lonely, and it's as bad as two. Two can also be lonely. This song has become a reality for some of my generation and has grown more believable as our culture has changed. This flagship song about the state of relationships between men and women is spot on today. Vast numbers of people are lonely. Some cannot form a relational bond, but as the song says; some relationships are as lonely as one.

It took less than ten years to explode back in the sixties. Something was going wrong. I was there but didn't recognize what "it" was until years later. Fortunately, I had already decided on a different path than many of my generation. But I did see the result of the deception.

"The Lie" replaced marriage, as designed by God, with loneliness. This song didn't mean much to me – I was never lonely. The song did address, in a way, how we humans are made. It has to do with the construction process of marriage. God designed marriage to work in three different areas. All that Satan and his world system had to do was monopolize a couple of unassociated events as we just saw, and he could pull off a revolution by eliminating one of these three parts of God's design. This old rock song was one of Satan's battle cries and still empowers his revolution today.

You may be thinking this song is not focused on marriage. True, this song did not have marriage in mind. Satan wants marriage removed from the picture. Marriage with a license is just a confining legal option that messes up his substitute schemes. Without a spiritual connection with God, man can be easily distracted from the truth.

This song is "on the mark" if you remove the way God builds things. The Master Designer said from the very beginning of His Creation, "Be fruitful and multiply." This means more than having children. God's plan is family. God wanted a Kingdom of people who were in His image and likeness. Embedded in our DNA, we have everything needed to carry out the mission. We were created to live together as a family. Satan has been working on his plan of loneliness for centuries. He started at the beginning trying to damage God's perfect design. As we move through the narrative, we will see that the key is that God builds with three parts.

The Master Designer knew that "one" was not enough. There is something about the way we are created that we must discover as we move through God's concept of marriage. The biblical facts are that a "man" has three parts. This has been lost to many today. We will look at this passage in Genesis Chapter 2:7 later. But my question is, do we have the street vocabulary to explain it?

Our first clue is found in Genesis 2:18 *And the Lord God said, It is not good that the man should be alone; I will make him an help meet for him.*

Did you see that scary word "alone?" Alone means unaccompanied, by yourself, and without help. God did not design us to be alone. Watching the Six O'clock News, we often hear about the atrocities committed by people who have isolated themselves. Being alone was never God's plan, but it is Satan's and his World System's objective. When we are alone, we are easier to manipulate.

What do I mean by manipulation? Have you ever heard of comfort food? When you are lonely, you are stuck with the "tube," the internet, a video game, or maybe a romance novel. With television, it is easy to see how it works. If you are lonely, your body has a way to help you change your emotions. It says, "Let's eat." And wouldn't you know, on the screen you are enticed with a large array of chips, cookies, ice cream or fast food - or the suggestion if you only had a new sexy car, the latest phone, or hottest fashion, you would have everything you want. Point: all these things still leave you alone.

God's plan of joy

Did you notice that Adam had God with him when Genesis 2:18 was stated? Adam was not alone; his Creator was with him. Nevertheless, God designed Adam for more. Adam needed a soul-mate. Our culture may not believe in soul-mates. The phrase is thought of as a mystical concept at best. Nevertheless, I find most couples who stay together know there is a deep connection with each other, even if they can't explain it. They just know.

But there is a problem. Two can be as lonely as one. It's the old rock song deal. And we must note, this is not God's design. It is interesting how the Creator made us in three unique components. See 1 Thessalonians 5:23 where Paul listed these three unique parts of men. He tells us about the physical body – this is how we relate to the earth. The soul is who we are - things like personality, knowledge, emotions, and desires. It is what we own for all eternity. He also tells us there is a spirit that connects us to God - but we all were born with a dead spirit because Adam died spiritually in the Garden and could not pass it on.

The fascinating thing is that He also used the same three areas as steps to building a permanent and joyful thing we call marriage. Using His plan is a form of assurance for success in the art of family. We might think of it as an "assurance policy."

We will see this plan develop and why we should know about it as we work our way through the ancient romance story. It is here we will see God's truth destroy all the deception about dating.

Three

My Story

My story is not needed, but you might want to know how I stumbled into living this old story. This story provided a form of insurance that has given me protection in my marriage. When I discovered this insurance policy in the Bible and the truth that is hidden in it, I was shocked. As a very young man, I had taken the path found in this narrative unknowingly. God had blessed my efforts of trusting in Him. It was many years later that I came face to face with what God had done in my life and the biblical desire that I pursued. As a University Sophomore, I was not anywhere near ready to think about marriage. Hence, I was not aggressively dating because I somehow knew that you marry the person you date. I knew that not dating equaled not marrying – I wasn't ready.

The five words "I want to be married" were not part of my world as I was growing up, during the Sixties. My mind was more on dreams like everybody else. As a kid, the goal was to be an astronaut or a scientist. Hey, we just put a man on the moon. Everybody was thinking big. I wasn't dreaming that BIG, but I did want to do something with my life that was worthwhile. That meant education. Marriage was not on my radar.

I had to balance this "Boomer" dreaming that "I could do anything" with another passion. I wanted to be involved in ministry. That was my plan from age thirteen. From the time I was saved at about age ten, I could see what God was doing. I had seen the amazing things happening week after week in the Church I attended. My plan was Bible College, but a free ride to the State University could not be turned down. This scholarship still worked with my life-plan since I never had the desire to be a vocational minister. I had asked God to give me a profession that would allow me to be involved with the Work of the Lord at my own expense. Not an astronaut, but a professional level job that left me time to be involved in ministry. I had no idea what this might mean, but I knew it was what I wanted.

You may be thinking I was a goofy teenager. But I had a plan, and it worked. So, I include a small snapshot of my story about my marriage.

I never thought about getting married, but I also never thought about staying single. I was a believer in God's Word and had no intention of stepping outside what He had commanded. I just wasn't dating; I was busy getting an education and starting a career.

Mathematics, Computers, and Drafting became my passion. I had no time for anything else. A friend and I started a business in my freshman year. I was on my way to living the dreams of a Boomer, and my plan to be involved in church ministry was still in my life-plan. And it all worked out because of the grace and mercy of The Lord Jesus Christ.

I did not walk away from my belief in God during those years at the State University, but I could have. Losing your focus on God is common at a higher educational institution. "Education" is the "god" they preach. My interest in God did move me to take a Religion "overview" class in my freshman semester. It met a "general education" requirement and was in the direction of my passion for Christ.

This class was almost a game changer. I had minimal difficulty rejecting any instructor or course filled with the liberal ideas that violated what I believed. This religion class, however, was taught by a man who was a Christian Minister. And by the end of the course, I wasn't sure about the Christian part. He taught four different worldwide religions with such equality that I wasn't sure which religious group he was connected.

I started to question my faith. If this professionally trained minister and university professor had no conviction about which religion was right, how could I know what to believe? By the end of the semester, the experience sent me searching for truth. And this search took some time.

What I found solidified my plans. The Bible I carried had no equal. I had the truth that had been proven correct for centuries in my hand. Some of the other religious systems he taught were vague in what they believed. They often varied in their primary doctrine which frequently changed over time. Some of these religious systems were recent in their arrival. My Bible had been unchanged and never proved wrong for thousands of years. And I might note, none of the other religious systems established a worldview that worked.

My faith survived instead of being shattered. But, so did my little experimental business. It was becoming very successful – I was earning a living on my own. The same was true for my education and undergraduate study and interest in Mathematics. I was starting to think and plan for a master's degree in Math. The Boomer dream was beginning to grow. Education was the key to success. I was living the dream.

And then I noticed her. The lack of interest or thinking about marriage started to change. The next year and a half of dating and engagement turned into what has now been almost fifty years of marriage as I write this book. What had happened in these eighteen months just happened, so I thought. It was years later that I realized God had led me down the Biblical path of dating, engagement, and marriage. I had never seen it or heard it taught. As we will see in the story of Isaac and Rebekah, God has a course of action that results in marriages that last. I did not realize at the time what had occurred. All I did was apply what little Bible I knew to my life. The one thing I understood was that God's ways were the right way. I didn't know what "right" was, but I knew what "wrong was." All I did was "resolve" in my heart to not do wrong. Years later I discovered that Daniel, the one in the lion's den, had done the same thing. He had *"purposed in his heart that he would not defile himself with the portion of the king's meat, nor with the wine which he drank:* (Dan 1:8).

Daniel experienced some things that were not so good. They changed his name to honor a pagan deity, and he received an education that could never be considered godly by anybody. Through it all, his choice for God's ways protected Daniel until he grew into his faith. My University experience was not, in any way, that horrible, but "The Lies" were everywhere, particularly on dating. I did not understand that my rejection of things that were "wrong" was all I needed to build a strong marriage based on God's principles – principles that I didn't even know. The big point here is that if you reject what you know is wrong, you have a chance of succeeding. If you do what you know is wrong, you lose.

So now I want to share what God has placed in various places throughout the Bible. We will focus on a story that I wish somebody had told me fifty years ago. God's Word has sure proved itself timeless. His ways to build a lifelong marriage are never changing.

And you would be right to think; I want to be married.

Some footnotes before we start: This book is perfect for those who are beginning the Dating Game. It also has things that parents with children need to teach. For those who have not had a good experience with dating or marriage, the principles are the same. It may require a retooling of the way you think, and how you approach this beautiful thing called marriage.

It will be worth it.

Special note here. The terms married, spouse and soul-mate,

will be used to identify a man and woman who married using God's plan in Genesis 2:24. Definitions of many words today have been changed to be gender neutral, but we will use the words as God has in the Bible.

The background is complete, so let's start this brilliant and romantic story found in the Book of Genesis. The romance may not be easily seen at first, but it is in the story.

Four

Isaac and Rebekah Their Story

An Encoded Guide to Dating, Engagement, and Marriage

I assume many of you have read the story in Genesis chapter twenty-four. If not, I have included all of it here. As we study our way through the story, we will find the "old way" of doing things "right." The secret is proving all things. You may question what this means, but we will all see soon enough. There is no short version of this story. Every word builds toward the point God is making. The story slowly teaches us what we need, one verse at a time.

> Gen 24:1-3 *And Abraham was old, and well stricken in age: and the Lord had blessed Abraham in all things. And Abraham said unto his eldest servant of his house, that ruled over all that he had, Put, I pray thee, thy hand under my thigh: And I will make thee swear by the Lord, the God of heaven, and the God of the earth, that thou shalt not take a wife unto my son of the daughters of the Canaanites, among whom I dwell:*

There are many Love stories in the Bible. The story of Ruth or the Song of Solomon are "love stories" - at least I think so.

But is the story of Isaac and Rebekah a "love story"? Or is it a story about an obsolete marriage practice - the "old way" of doing things? Most might say it is a great tale from the "old days," but with little application today. This old narrative shows how Isaac and Rebekah came together in marriage. If you know the narrative, I can hear you thinking, "What has this to do with dating?" I suggest it has everything to do with dating. Despite the fact, get ready for this, dating is not in the Bible, nor is the concept of dating.

What we see in Genesis Twenty-four is known as an "arranged marriage," a practice that has been the way of the world for most of recorded history. The fathers arranged the marriage. In this story about Isaac and Rebekah, we will see how it "used to work." On the other hand, I want to show you how the same principles apply to the current process of dating.

In the first few verses of Genesis 24, you might notice several things are missing from the current Boomers' inspired concept of dating and marriage. I am referring to "dating for fun," and not getting married but just living together. Of course, what we are going to see is God's way. God's concepts have been lost in the deception I call "The Lie." You will notice in the first few words that old men with wisdom are very much part of this old story. This was not just any information, but wisdom based on spiritual truth.

What is the history of dating?

History is extremely important because we don't have enough time to make all the mistakes our ancestors made again. That is the message hiding in the first few words of Gen 24:1. We need the wisdom of old men who have been there, bought the tee-shirt and worn it out. They know what mistakes not to make. We should pay attention to old wisdom.

We saw some of these mistakes in the Generational Divide chapter. This is a cultural and historical background we need to understand. Dating today is a cultural thing, starting mainly in American society at the start of 1900, the Twentieth Century. Dating is the process where two people randomly meet and explore the possibility of marriage with no rules, no experience and no assistance from wisdom necessary. Don't miss the no-rules part. It is just "do what you want." The process is physically and emotionally driven. And the process is disconnected from the real purpose of marriage.

Throughout history, and currently in most parts of the world, young people might meet while working or in group settings - IF, and it is a big IF, they meet at all. Worldwide, marriages have been and are still often "arranged." This "arranged" process is a very Biblical concept if the union is arranged by God as we will see in our coming story. Unfortunately, arranged marriages in history quickly fell prey to private parental agendas. While full of complications and pitfalls, the old process may be better than our current dating process. Do not think for a moment I am suggesting we go back – I'm not. But you must agree that the present method of dating leaves much to be desired.

God's plans transcend culture. His principles always apply to all people in all cultures. While the word or concept of dating is not found in the Bible, if God is allowed into the process, the results will lead to success. It's in the story of Isaac and Rebekah. Let's start by exposing a little piece of trickery that the "purpose" of dating is only to have fun. This should not be the approach and is potentially dangerous. Dating may be a fun activity. But no matter how you approach dating, the ultimate purpose is to find a mate. The process of dating is more than a way to "fit in" or to make people think you are popular. Dating is not just a way to have a good time and get out of the house.

Here is my point as down to earth as I can say it: if you don't date the wrong people, – you won't marry the wrong people. You can quote me on this – I worked hard trying to figure this out.

Every one of the sixty-seven verses in Genesis 24 will give us spiritual wisdom needed in the process of dating. I am using the word "dating" to mean the process of finding your soul-mate. I am just skipping a stone across this compelling story to show you how God has encoded what we need to know as we move into the process of marriage.

The truth we are hunting for is here. The following material is to help us see how to apply the Word of God by comparing Scripture to Scripture to help us use the truth in our situation.

We join the story of Abraham right after he buried Sarah, his wife of many years. Sarah was Isaac's mother. A difficult time for husband and son. Death has the effect of re-directing our thinking about life. Time is short on this earth, and things must be done before it is too late.

Gen 24:1 *And Abraham was old, and well stricken in age: and the Lord had blessed Abraham in all things.*

What has old and stricken in age to do with Marriage? Age should bring wisdom.

Notice that the "Lord had blessed Abraham in all things." What we have here is code for us to pay attention. Remember why God had blessed Abraham. James told us about it in James 2:23. Abraham believed God - he was called the friend of God. Now Abraham was old and concerned about his son Isaac because he needed a wife. Not just any woman, but the one God would choose. Here is a biblical truth: when choosing a soul-mate, you need to use Old Wisdom.

Abraham had a long marriage to his wife, Sarah. Through the years, mistakes were made by both. But they stayed together through it all. She was central in his life, and he understood marriage. He knew what to look for in Isaac's future wife. No mistakes allowed here. Abraham was too old physically to personally carry out the task. So, he turned to the one he trusted most - an unnamed servant.

Few people in our culture would like the "old way" where the father decides who marries who. I get this because there is a built-in issue. For this process to work, it requires parents to be walking with God. They must be tracking with God. It is more than possible, as we saw when we went backstage with the generational rift, parents may not be thinking God's way. There is always a chance for that private agenda thing.

Nevertheless, parents should be involved in the process we now call dating. Involvement by Mom and Dad with underage children is mandatory. Dating too young will result in nothing but pain that will be carried throughout life. Arranged marriages from the old day had a better chance of working than modern dating when we consider the baggage created by improper dating. Baggage that a person has with him his whole life.

Gen 24:2 *And Abraham said unto his eldest servant of his house, that ruled over all that he had, Put, I pray thee, thy hand under my thigh*:

This eldest servant's name is Eliezer (Gen 15:2). Why didn't God just name him? Wouldn't that have been easier? We cannot claim to know why God works the way He works, but we can discover some possibilities. In Genesis 12:4 we see that his servant named Eliezer was going to be Abraham's only heir. At that time Abraham had no children, even though God had promised his seed would become a great nation. As you read the passage notice that Abraham had total faith in this man to carry out a mission that he could not do personally. That kind of trust results from years of faithful interaction in all things. Best guess for me is the unnamed servant is Eliezer.

The single most important thing that Abraham had to do at this place in his life was seeing that his bloodline, his seed, would continue as God had promised. It was the father's job to oversee the process. Since there was no such thing as dating in those days, it was up to Abraham. Time was now beginning to close in on Abraham, so he used the most trusted resource he had - an unnamed servant.

We may not be sure about the identity of the unnamed servant. But by default, this job, must be carried out by Eliezer.

It was too important for just anybody. We will generally use the name Eliezer in place of the title "unnamed servant." All commentaries seem to agree on this. As we will see, this deep relationship they had is needed by the type of oath used in the story. Abraham trusted this man.

There is no reason to think Eliezer's name was unknown to the writer of this story. My guess is he did not use Eliezer's name because God has encoded a spiritual message inside of this historical event. There is a picture being painted in the background. Abraham was the "father" and spiritually pictures God the Father. When we add the unnamed servant, we can see a hidden figure in God's bigger story. Unnamed is a lot like being unseen. Always present and silently serving, but not seen or called by name. The unnamed Servant would picture the Holy Spirit. Yes, as you may have already guessed, the Holy Spirit is very much part of this story of a marriage. If the writer used Eliezer's name, this hidden code or beautiful picture would be lost.

What we are seeing is how the unseen Spirit of God functions. The Holy Spirit that indwells believers serves by directing our way toward the truth and the correct answers to any problems we may face. This is unseen and happens without the exchange of words or names. The Holy Spirit of truth silently provides what we need when we need it. The Holy Spirit can be trusted more than anything else in our lives. We will see this Spirit of Truth in many places as we move through this story. Each step requires spiritual guidance. Marriage is a very critical part of life. God should be involved in every area of it.

This Power of the Holy Spirit is seldom mentioned in the social-church today. Like I have already said, this power is lost in "The Lie's" substitute theory that says man has only two parts. The unseen Spirit of God has been left out of the conversation in our culture in general. For many today, the Spirit of God is some mystical and magical thing. They leave God's Spirit out of the process. But God the Father and Jesus do not leave the Holy Spirit out of the story. As we move through these verses, I will try to show you how the Holy Spirit can be very real – not some hocus pocus mysterious thing that cannot be understood.

The "hand under the thigh" is a bizarre thing at best. However, with very little meditation it is easy to see what the old and archaic custom is telling us. It moves our modern mind to sexual thoughts. And that is one part of the purpose. This oath and physical location of hand under another's thigh focuses our attention on the ultimate result of this process. Abraham's plan was focused on the future of the family – and sexuality is in the process of family. The method of the oath used showed his servant the purpose and, at the same time, his trust. It is as if Abraham is transferring his functionality as a father to his servant to seek out the bride. To allow this oath took an extremely high level of trust with the hand's location. This ritual shows a personal and intimate faith in their relationship. The point is simple: Abraham trusted Eliezer to carry out the mission of finding Isaac's bride.

The process of finding Isaac's wife is a monumentally important task. This woman would be the mother of Abraham's generations to come. Ultimately, she is in the bloodline of the Savior of the world. The same is true for the person you are to marry. Your life is also important to God. Only the perfect answer will do. God is not a respecter of persons. His desire for you is nothing but the best.

I wonder how many times a couple thinks about what I just said. Why do believers who trust God for their eternal life, see no value in his infinite wisdom in choosing a lifelong soul-mate? Has the world's idea that lust is the only driving force behind marriage taken over? Is lust the only motivator considered? That seems to be the new rule of marriage. Keep these Hollywood schemes in mind as we continue. The marketing technique of "you can do better" is nothing more than fuel for lust. God's ways of forming a lifelong relationship of marriage are very different than anything you will watch on any screen.

Genesis 24 will show us that parents and others were involved – it is not a solo thing. We will see practical examples of the godly method for our culture found in the old process of arranged marriages. Examples we can use today. One of the first is that Rebekah was from the right family.

> Gen 24:3 *And I will make thee swear by the Lord, the God of heaven, and the God of the earth, that thou shalt not take a wife unto my son of the daughters of the Canaanites, among whom I dwell.*

This story will lead us to God's answer, and is full of details and advice, like where to look for your soul-mate. It includes a warning. Don't search for your soul-mate in places where you do not want to be. Most people get their Bible knowledge from little tidbits here and there and use their imagination from context to make up what they do not know. Unfamiliar readers with the story would guess that daughters of the Canaanites were a wrong choice. And that would be true.

But why?

Our imagination directed by movies would suggest they were ugly, bad mothers, uneducated, culturally backward, unfaithful or just not desirable. Biblically these things are not seen in the Scriptures. There is, however, an issue that takes them off the search list. They had been convinced and thoroughly brainwashed into believing in "do-nothing-gods" made by men from wood and stone.

For generations, the Canaanites had been taught they must manipulate pieces of wood (false gods) into being kind to them. The blocks of carved wood did not move or speak; in fact, they never did anything, but the Canaanites were heart and soul dedicated to these fake gods. There are very few cases where any- body from this culture of idolatry ever escaped their desire to manipulate the "do-nothing-gods." (Rahab, in Joshua 2:1 – 6:25, is a rare exception.) Their belief in manipulation became so addictive that they would sacrifice their children to these useless gods in the hope of obtaining favors from them. This "lie" is fueled by the handlers of these false gods who benefited greatly by the false doctrine.

It was not just the peoples' false believe in idols but the "thought" they could manipulate them that made them un-redeemable. The Creator of the universe is not to be managed. We have all seen it before. There is a point where sin will hold an entire culture captive, and God's only answer, as with Sodom and Gomorrah, is to permanently remove them and stop the spread of their addiction to evil.

These do-nothing-gods and handlers still exist today. Legal and illegal drugs have their pushers. Alcohol has its bars, and we find stacks of bottles and cans of alcohol located in most places we go. And then there are the things that can be seen on the Internet. The marketplace is trying to sell products that do nothing except give a few minutes of escape from stress and loneliness. It is the same hope that the do-nothing-gods gave back in the day. Pay me a small token, and I might do what you want. These fake gods can look like a big house, expensive cars, a career move, or maybe the Hollywood fantasy, "If I could look like that, I could get what I want." People spend too much time trying to become whatever the media is pushing at the time.

Are you getting the idea that maybe following do-nothing-gods, like the media, might not be the parameters that we should apply in a search for a soul mate? But Abraham's years of wisdom said, "Don't search here." Abraham knew there was one place that might have the right kind of person needed to carry out God's plan.

Gen 24:4 *But thou shalt go unto my country, and to my kindred, and take a wife unto my son Isaac.*

One thing Abraham knew was that there were no suitable women in the land of Canaan. And he should know, he had spent years there. Sounds like a good plan, going back home.

But, we know from future stories in the Bible, going back home to find a wife, by itself, is not enough to guarantee success. Idolatry was active in Abraham's old country also, and Abraham knew this. In fact, it is the same land of idolatry that Abraham walked away from when he began seeking God's unidentified place for himself.

Don't get the idea there is a place to go that has fully stocked sections of the "right" person. But then again God knew there was one girl who was a virtuous woman in the making, and she was in Abraham's old home place. It indeed was a better choice than the hopeless Canaanites. All God had to do was move Abraham into thinking. And that thought took him back home to his people. It was a good plan.

Five

IF DATING IS NOT A BIBLICAL CONCEPT, WHERE DID WE GET IT?

Gen 24:4-9 *But thou shalt go unto my country, and to my kindred, and take a wife unto my son Isaac. And the servant said unto him, Peradventure the woman will not be willing to follow me unto this land: must I needs bring thy son again unto the land from whence thou camest?*

And Abraham said unto him, Beware thou that thou bring not my son thither again. The Lord God of heaven, which took me from my father's house, and from the land of my kindred, and which spake unto me, and that sware unto me, saying, Unto thy seed will I give this land; he shall send his angel before thee, and thou shalt take a wife unto my son from thence. And if the woman will not be willing to follow thee, then thou shalt be clear from this my oath: only bring not my son thither again. And the servant put his hand under the thigh of Abraham, his master, and sware to him concerning that matter.

World War One is where we find the introduction that started it all, and World War Two completed the new "dating concept," a concept that left parents out of the process. In both World Wars, young men were sent to fight the war.

Particularly in World War Two, the need to manufacture military equipment far exceeded the ability of the men left back at home. What was needed was an additional workforce to fill the gap. With many men gone, women stepped into the workforce in a big way, and things begin to change. Instead of being home under their father's watchful eye, they were out on their own. They no longer had to depend on dad - financially or emotionally.

Parental responsibility slowly eroded away. Independence in the workplace led to freedom in marriage. This first step away from parental wisdom to lust was slow - but it was a big step away. The Roaring Twenties demonstrated the start of free choice without always making sense.

It is about time we uncover more of the trickery that the purpose of dating is only to have fun.

Roller Coasters are fun. You get a thrill, and maybe an upset stomach. With random, careless physical-based dating, you may get something much worse than an upset stomach. As with the excitement of a roller coaster, there are a lot of ups and downs and doubt. No, that wasn't a typographical error. I said doubt. It is perhaps leading to a lifetime of doubt.

Say, for example, you and the person you were dating went too far physically, and you end up eventually marrying. What you did while "dating" may have implanted doubt and lack of trust in the marriage.

You both know what each is capable of doing. Trusting your spouse may remain under that "dark cloud" of doubt. If some- body went too far outside of marriage once, will they do it again? Doubt can keep the union from working. Physical dating gives Satan the powerful built-in tool of doubt in which to work you. And that can become an issue more often than you think possible. Suspicion damages the essential element of marriage called trust. Oneness will suffer, and marriage could easily fail without trust.

I am not saying this happens in all cases. I am just saying if dating is done God's way, the marriage will start with a considerable level of trust. Otherwise, trust must be built over time. I saw this happen to others in a marriage years ago. They seemed to live with constant suspicion that their spouse was cheating on them. There did not seem to be a reason other than the way they started their marriage.

Dating with wisdom.

If the dating experience is group dating, then there is built-in protection from the flesh taking over. This is extremely important for teens, but it is also a practical, safeguard for starting first dates for all ages. Most churches have activities that can also be used to get to know somebody. These can make a great first date experience.

What do I mean by group dating? A group date is a time spent getting to know each other without a commitment to an implied relationship. You have time and opportunities to prove that there is a spiritual attraction — time to see if God is in the process. Church activities, small groups, going out to get ice cream any situation that does not automatically label the activity as a commitment. Avoiding the social "image" of being a couple removes the pain of breaking up. If the spiritual attraction is present, finding "safe" places and things to do together will become very obvious to both.

Group dating is a great way to start, providing the group is doing things God's way. Being in the wrong crowd, at the wrong place, at the wrong time could be worse than "solo" dating. The group could drag you down before you see it coming. Peer pressure is a powerful thing. When situations are not allowed to become physical, then dating can lead to a godly marriage.

The most prominent danger is for teens who do not have the ability to understand the threat of a relationship based only on the physical. A spiritual relationship must be built first. The physical side of marriage comes later.

Gen 24:5 *And the servant said unto him, Peradventure the woman will not be willing to follow me unto this land: must I needs bring thy son again unto the land from whence thou camest?*

I see this as an unexpected question. "What if," the unnamed servant asks, "the woman doesn't want to leave her land?" Do you see the freedom here? Marriage must be something both parties want. There can be no pretense. There is no trickery allowed. The servant was a trusted servant. That meant he was not just to bring back a girl, but he was to bring back the correct girl. As we read this story, notice that everything was upfront and honest. There was no matchmaking with exaggerated stories about the groom to be.

As we move forward, we will find some situations in which we might try to insert some of our contemporary thoughts into the story. For example, we might want to suppose that Rebekah wanted to get married so she would not have to carry water for the family. Carrying water is hard work. We also might see the expensive jewelry that turns up in the story as being an enticement to trick her into marriage. But from context, we will clearly see that these ideas are not the case. We must let the story explain itself and not add outside ideas to see what we need to learn about God, dating, and marriage. What we find is a God-given example on how a marriage should start.

Rebekah speaks for herself. We will see "why" she agreed, which is what the servant now wants to know, "What if this woman doesn't want to be part of this spiritual family?" The answer to "why" she said yes is the key to understanding successful dating. The last part of the question was "What if I must take Isaac there to convince her?" Remember this was a "sight unseen" marriage. The jewelry, given by itself, would not "move" many women into marriage. You might expect that Rebekah would also have a "what if" moment. What if he was too old, deformed, or - well, you can use your imagination. Remember she only saw the servants. And if it wasn't money, why would she say yes? We will learn the gifts were not given to impress Rebekah. Keep your eyes open for indicators of what was motivating Rebekah. With Hollywood's standards deeply rooted in our minds, and with the many miles that separated them we can't insert the usual physical attraction as motivation, but we also must fight the urge to think the appeal is only money. We must read carefully to see what Rebekah's motivation is. Why would she do this?

What is the message for us? There must be the rightreasons to marry. As with Rebekah, it should not be appearance or money. What we are starting to do is build a checklist of what we should be looking for and what should be avoided.

Gen 24:6 *And Abraham said unto him, Beware thou that thou bring not my son thither again.*

Flag down on the play, stop the game. Abraham knew without thinking that his son could not go back to his old home. Why wouldn't Abraham let his son go back to his homeland? Did Dad know something that we don't know? I already told you that idolatry was alive and well in Abraham's homeland. But I didn't fill you in on some stuff about idol worship.

Do-nothing-gods built from wood and stone are - well, boring. They do nothing. A block of wood or a piece of rock only sits where it is placed. Unless it is picked up and moved, nothing ever happens. At best they are just run-of-the-mill art pieces. Being boring becomes a problem, so their handlers had to find something to make them interesting. They added some "glitz." You must have an audience to make money, and "glitz" will build an audience.

I know believers don't like the word "worship" used in this fashion. But worship means transferring worth to something. Worth-is-shipped is an excellent way to think of worship. The world "worships" Rock stars and actors and actresses. They have the glitz, and they bring in the money.

So, the false priests (idol handlers) had to add something to increase the value of their wooden blocks and hunks of rock. If you will put your thinking hat on and analyze our television and movie industry, you will know what the media's main objective is. It is the same as the idol handlers – keeping an audience watching so the industry can stay in business - they bring on the "glitz."

How many times can a sitcom play the same gag, and people not lose interest? Even the Three Stooges got boring, and back in their day, they had little competition. So, what do those who seek advertising dollars do to keep their ratings? Think Jeopardy music here. The answer is from the "Catch Your Eye category" or "Illicit Sex and Useless Violence category." The question is, "What kind of glitz does it take to hold an audience during primetime TV?"

Back in Abraham's days with the gods of wood and stone, life was hard. Violence would not play so well. Consequently, sexuality outside of marriage became the glitz. God called it prostitution because it was. Very few details are given in the Bible because the word "prostitution" is all you need to know. There are some things a person must avoid contact with because they are extremely toxic and dangerous - particularly in the context of marriage. Prostitution, which includes pornography, is such a thing. Abraham wanted his son to stay in the safety of family, and not out in the world looking to see what glitz he might see.

Just a note: It depends on what translation you read, but most modern translations use the word prostitution. The KJV might use phrases like "strange women, whore, or harlot." But it is easy to see that prostitution is connected to idolatry in more biblical texts than I can list. God didn't go into detail, and I am going to stop with this simple point. There were reasons Abraham did not want his son out and about looking for a wife in Canaan or the land in which he once lived.

Did you get the significant subtle warning here? It is not that hard to see. Where are you looking for that "right person?" Is the answer at the local bar or nightclub? And if so, what kind of person are you looking to find in this kind of nightspot? Your godly soul-mate would never be looking for you in these kinds of places. There is nothing there you want in your marriage. The message: Stay out of Canaan. Satan's glitz could sidetrack you for a lifetime. Father Abraham knew this well.

This marriage is one of the most important in the Bible – just like your marriage is one of the most essential things in your story. Here is why:

> Gen 12:1-3: *Get thee out of thy country, and from thy kindred, and from thy father's house, unto a land that I will shew thee: And I will make of thee a great nation, and I will bless thee, and make thy name great; and thou shalt be a blessing: And I will bless them that bless thee, and curse him that curseth thee: and in thee shall all families of the earth be blessed.*

Back in Chapter Twelve, Abraham did not know where he was going, but he left for this unknown place by faith. Faith should be thought of as trusting the Lord. We can now see, all these years later, that being in the land had great value to Abraham. Being where God wants you is essential. Oh, I think I just wrote something important.

When Abraham left the Promised Land and went to Egypt because of a lack of faith, things did not go well. You can read about it in the balance of Chapter Twelve. I have found that trusting God is a faith builder. By Genesis Chapter 15 we see that Abraham's faith was strong. He believed, and the Lord God counted it to him for righteousness.

You may ask what this has to do with dating. It is called faith. Do you believe that the God who provided a way for you to have eternal life through His Son Jesus could also provide you with the perfect soul mate? Since I was not actively looking, it surprised me when I recognized that I might have found her. Unknowingly, I used the same spiritual process we are going to see in this chapter about Isaac and Rebekah. Faith in God is a big part of the process.

The phrase, "I will make you a great nation" probably

doesn't make our hearts skip a beat. Our culture tends to look at temporary things. We as a culture focus on a good expensive cup of coffee, the next blockbuster movie, or getting to the next level of the latest video game. Building a family is seldom top priority in our society's plans. I suspect that if the text said God promised Abraham the advance release of the next version of the I-Phone, somebody out there would say cool, I want to be Abraham. "The Lie" has turned upside down the old values, and our culture has lost the glue that keeps families together.

I'm a Baby Boomer, and I love technology as much as anybody. And I will openly admit that it was not my goal to have a great nation of children. But now fifty years later with teenage grandchildren, I get it. I have seen the big movies, I have had the great "toys," and the coffee was good, but not one of those thrills lasted more than a few minutes. But the family is different. Stay with me, and I will point out what God is doing as we go through this story.

There are some significant points made in Genesis 24:7. The first explains why Abraham did not want Isaac to go back to his homeland. My comments about idolatry may have been in the back of Abraham's mind, but Abraham had experienced God's blessing and seen the curse against his enemies work many times. But in verse seven we know God spoke to Abraham about this process. If you take out some of the stuff inserted with commas, it is easy to see: The Lord God of heaven ... which spake unto me, and that sware unto me, Unto thy seed will I give this land. God's promise to Abraham connects him to the land. The place God put Abraham has unique value to God. Check me out on this, almost everything in the Bible that is good and of any significance takes place inside the land that God gave to Abraham.

That includes the Cross, the Resurrection, and His return.

So where are you? The place God wants you? God does not make mistakes. We are the ones who make mistakes.

Gen 24:7 *The Lord God of heaven, which took me from my father's house, and from the land of my kindred, and which spake unto me, and that sware unto me, saying, Unto thy seed will I give this land; he shall send his angel before thee, and thou shalt take a wife unto my son from thence.*

This verse gives us some crucial information. It tells us that the Lord God has sent his angel ahead of the caravan. Without question, we are seeing God's involvement in this marriage. We will investigate this, but first, Abraham gives us a little history. He tells us the Lord took him from his father's house and moved his family into a promised land. The story is found in Genesis Chapter Twelve. The text says that Abraham was given "a command" with a promise, a blessing, and built-in protection from God. Abraham was 75 years old when this happened.

Some believers may not think that God speaks to them. That is wrong thinking. God has many ways of communication; the most common is through his Written Word with the aid of the Holy Spirit.

Reading the Bible is one of the best ways. Even a few minutes reading the Bible each day can change your life. It seems reasonable that people who love God would want to know about Him. It is like a marriage. A biblical marriage is nothing like what present culture teaches. It is much more. I still find my wife of fifty years fascinating. I love to hear her talk about what has happened during the day. Soul-mates grow closer each day be- cause they care about each other. They seek information about each other.

It takes less than 80 hours to read the Bible from cover to cover, which is only about fifteen minutes of your time each day to read the Bible in a year. That is less time than the annoying commercials in any given hour of television. Where do you give your time?

If you are not happy with your life, then do something

different. If what you are doing is not working - don't' do it. Like the doctor's answer to your complaint, "It hurts when I do this" – don't do it. If you struggle with reading the KJV, then I might suggest a more contemporary version. I have read many different translations and paraphrased versions. At times, while reading, they have sent me back to the KJV, and I see something new that I had never noticed before. Comparing Scripture with Scripture includes translation to translation. I know this takes time. But remember, it is not about the volume of words you read. Strive for understanding. If you spend ten minutes and comprehend what you read in one verse, that may be better than reading an entire chapter.

God, in the Scriptures, often communicated with Abraham through The Angel of the Lord. This is seen with others in the Old Testament. How God communicates is not essential if we get the message. His primary method today is through His Written Word. But it might come from a Pastor, a mentor, a friend, or a song on Christian radio. In the Old Testament there were some intriguing ways such as a burning bush or a talking donkey. Don't be looking for this kind of communication, but God will get His message to you if you keep your spiritual eyes open. The process of Dating, Engagement, and Marriage are worth doing right. In this story with Abraham, The Lord God sent an angel before Eliezer. It will most likely be the same for you except it will be His Indwelling Spirit that will be preparing the way.

The last major thing we need to look at here is the statement "send his angel before thee." Our culture talks a lot about angels. Most of the talk you hear has nothing to do with what the Word of God has to say about angels. In this case, we don't know who this angel is or what the angel did.

The word angel means messenger. In places, we know the name of a few angel messengers like Gabriel and Michael. And we know The Angel of the Lord turns up on a few occasions in the Old Testament. God's angels are mentioned in many places, but as with this passage, little is told about what they do. In this case with Abraham, we know the results. If I was to speculate, I think what this angel did was spiritual work. Perhaps this messenger was the Holy Spirit who took the spiritual message to Rebekah and her family. This is my wild guess. But the thought does fit. We know the Spirit of God at the time of Creation moved upon the face of the waters in Genesis 1:2, and the Holy Spirit is involved in the process of Salvation.

The Angel of the Lord did pave the way for the "trip." He did talk to Abraham and told him he was going to send an angel ahead to prepare the way. We have no details about this. We don't know what this angel did, but we will see the result that he arranged.

Gen 24:8 *And if the woman will not be willing to follow thee, then thou shalt be clear from this my oath: only bring not my son thither again.*

We now hear the unnamed servant's question. What if he locates this woman and she will not come? Abraham is trusting that God will do what He says. Here is the point; Abraham is not demanding those who are helping him do what only God can do. But that's what some people expect. They want somebody else to solve their problems. Only God alone can resolve some kinds of glitches. You must trust Him and let Him do His work.

There is a hidden point here. Don't expect somebody to solve your marital issues outside of God.

Marriage is about two people who desire marriage. It is to be made with free choice and based on what each of the two wants to do; physically, it has failure written all over it unless God's truth fuels the marriage. Free-will must have the correct information to make the right decision. Abraham let his servant off the hook. If the woman God selected did not want to follow his servant back to Isaac, Eliezer was relieved of his oath.

Thinking of the unnamed servant as the unseen Holy Spirit, we see a connection to God's truth. God does not make anyone do things His way – it is their choice. So here is a question, what if the "right" person is not tracking with God? In terms of free-will, the Spirit of God may not succeed. The Spirit of God moves, and this goes for you and the one for whom you are looking. Success is when your soul-mate sees in you what you must see in them. There are many things that Rebekah saw that stirred her to say yes. These same things will become evident as you learn to look with spiritual eyes. If you use only "physical cues," you will never see the things you must see.

> Gen 24:9 *And the servant put his hand under the thigh of Abraham, his master, and sware to him concerning that matter.*

When God starts repeating something, He wants to make sure you do not miss the BIG points. The oath and physical location of hand under another's thigh should move our attention to the expected result of this process - family. The father's desire is a family, and that starts with spiritual roots. Roots are something that will last. If you think God has no interest in you, then why would He allow His Son to die for you? God desires the best for you, but you must also want the best.

What is God's plan for marriage?

Six

THE LOST DEFINITION

We need to step out of the story for a second and make sure we understand Biblical marriage. Let's start with the Biblical definition of marriage. Marriage is often taught from the situations a teacher/preacher has experienced. It may also depend on the person to whom he is speaking. What we want to believe and what the Bible says may not be the same. Our objective is not to find "liberties" in the Bible but to read and understand what the Bible says. God's Word is pure. This topic is straightforward and easy to comprehend. The thing that makes dating and marriage hard is when the wrong definitions are used. Inadequate definitions lead to bad results.

What are your definitions of dating and marriage, and where did you get them? I'll make up some samples.

- Dating is a way to have fun.

- Dating proves how popular I am.

- Marriage is a permanent way to escape the process of dating. (I guess because dating is not much fun?)

- Marry quickly because the biological clock is ticking away.

But what is your definition? Here is what the Urban on-line Dictionary says – you are going to like this! I did not make this up.

Dating is where two people, who are attracted to each other, spend time together to see if they also can stand to be around each other most of the time. If this is successful, they develop a relationship. However, sometimes a relationship develops anyways if the people can't find anybody else to date. In some cases, one or the other is very lonely, or, one person is only attracted to the other and pretends to be in love. The unfortunate misled person has the misunderstanding that they have found love. This scenario of misunderstood love occurs quite often and eventually leads to something called cheating.

It's a sure bet your mental definition of marriage is from the way you were raised. The Media generally establishes lifestyle in this country. We watch "violent action movies" and say it is just fiction, yet we become desensitized to real death and violence. It's the new normal to see body parts and blood fly all around. Violence is nothing to us. Somebody shoots up an elementary school, and we no longer react with grief for the innocent lives lost by a confused mind that has seen nothing but violence as the path to getting what it wants.

The same is true for dating and marriage. We watch hours and hours of programming showing relationship situations based on lust. We try to say that the circumstances in these shows and movies are just fiction - yet we allow them to influence our way of thinking.

Definition of Marriage

The definition is always the most critical part of any controversial study. A faulty interpretation can provide many useful sounding and logical conclusions that may not be true to an accurate definition. No description of marriage will be satisfactory in our study other than God's definition. God's explanation is found in the first mention of the concept in the Bible.

> Gen 2:24: *Therefore shall a man **leave** his father and his mother, and shall **cleave** unto his wife: and they shall be **one** flesh.*

Notice, there are three parts – This is what we should now expect. God builds things in threes. The definition of marriage has three components. They match the three parts of man (body, soul, and spirit) which are in the image of the Father, Son, and Holy Spirit. You might guess that when God defined marriage, he connected it to the three parts of man on purpose.

- "One flesh" refers to the physical body – the part of marriage that everybody understands.

- "Leave" refers to the soul which is the seat of our emotions– it is a key part of marriage. Leaving the family you were raised in is a very emotional thing.

- "Cleave" is the spiritual connection. We do not see it, but it is there. It is by faith that God ordained marriage for life.

The definition provided in Genesis has never changed. It is in a Hebrew perspective in Matthew 19:5-6 and Mark 10:8, and with a Church focus in Ephesian 5:31. We find the "cleave" part clearly in Matthew.

> Matt 19:5,6 *And said, For this cause shall a man **leave** father and mother, and shall **cleave** to his wife: and they twain shall **be one flesh**? Wherefore they are no more twain, but one flesh. What therefore God **hath joined together**, let not man put asunder.*

The word "cleave" was also translated in the KJV as: abide fast, joined (together), and stick. Abide means: remain, stay, reside (the same words are used to explain a relationship with God –

it's a spiritual word). Emotions come and go, and the physical is always temporary, but cleave shows permanence. Strong's dictionary second definition is to stick fast, adhere or cling.

The question is: How can I be glued to someone?

The Etymology is fascinating. It takes us back to clay. It was God who glued clay together to get Adam. Cleave has two entirely different definitions. The one we have seen – to adhere and the other to "divide by blow." Was it not God that divided Adam to get Eve? God was involved in marriage from day one. But modern man ignores this fact.

So, how are we "glued" to someone? Physical and emotional bonds can and do change. But God said, "Shall cleave." It is God's spiritual "glue" that places together those God designed for each other. Trace the word "cleave" through the Bible and see God's involvement.

Cleave seems to be the word God used to explain His part in marriage. It is the part we cannot take apart. Seeking God's direction in marriage is very important. The result is a covenant relationship based on trust. This concept of a marriage covenant is a casualty of the sixties' "free love" movement. A marriage covenant is binding. If Satan could get rid of the covenant's binding component, then marriages could be freely broken by anybody anytime. Result: you get "love songs" about being lonely – it's a package deal with no options.

A covenant is different than a contract. A contract can be evaluated on performance. A covenant is an agreement with no conditional requirements. This is easy to understand in view of God's plan for unconditional love. Our culture has replaced the word covenant with the word "contract." This is a horrible mistake. Contracts have performance clauses, which allow them to be broken. And that is not part of God's plan for marriage. Like the old saying goes, "The devil is in the details," but words are important to God. What God says is what He means.

This change in wording allowed a major step to take place

without notice. The removal of a marriage contract back with the Boomers in the sixties changed everything. I doubt if Satan or his World System had a clue what this would do to a Christian Society. And I am sure he didn't care. What he got was a complete collapse of the infrastructure that made this country great. He won a great victory while everybody lost the critical relationship known as family. Loneliness had taken over.

Biblical Marriage is a covenant relationship. The word "covenant" means agreement, undertaking, commitment, guarantee, warrant, pledge, promise, arrangement, or understanding. A covenant relationship is more than a simple contract. It is a lifelong oath, a commitment that is not to be altered. It is a solemn promise between two parties that is impossible to break.

People who made covenants in the Old Testament often slaughtered animals to demonstrate what must happen to break the covenant. Death was the only way such an agreement could be broken.

The thought of an unbreakable covenant is not part of marriage in our society today. An unbreakable "contract" is a foreign concept in the current American world view. It's hard to get people to sign a simple contract for a new cell phone for a year. You often see this with popular advertisements – no contract needed. Even short-term agreements are considered bad news. The word "covenant" is seldom heard.

Satan must be beaming with evil joy. A covenant is the backbone of God's relationship with His Creation. God made a covenant with all mankind, and He will keep His part. Some of the daily problems we experience are the result of somebody not keeping their side of an agreement. A man's word should be the same as the man. God's Word is always consistent with who He is. He always keeps His Word, and you cannot tell God apart from His Word. But today, men's words mean nothing; they change with the wind.

Because people do not trust each other, we now have the

21st-century hatred for any contract, and this certainly applies to a marriage covenant. Some want the freedom to change, but this lack of commitment throws out the concept of trust, which is what marriage is all about. God's part of marriage, "cleaving" is all but lost in the modern and faulty way of thinking. The final point here came from Jesus: *What God hath joined together, let not man put asunder.*

These three critical parts of marriage will turn up everywhere in this story.

- "Be one flesh" is the physical relationship.

- "Leaving" is the soul part of marriage.

- "Cleave" is God's part of the marriage covenant.

One variation of "The Lie" is that men and women are the same. Anybody who has raised a family with both boys and girls will tell you this is just not true. They are very different from birth, and it is not just about how we treat them. God made them different. When God told Adam, he needed a help-meet God knew what he was saying. A husband and wife team play and build upon their strengths and weaknesses. It was God's plan, and it works well when we do not interfere with it.

Back to the story of Rebekah

In the story of Isaac and Rebekah, the groundwork had been set in place, and so the journey began. We will now discover that this was not some casual and unplanned undertaking. Every possible thing to guarantee success had been put into motion. There is a truth hidden here for us today – dating is to be a serious activity. Dating is something that should not just happen. It should be planned.

When dating is approached only as "fun" the result is different than if dating is viewed as the path to marriage. If the person you are dating is not someone you want to be joined to for life, they are not soul-mate material. Why risk a date on something you know will not work? Don't lie to yourself when a dating mistake is obvious before it starts.

> Gen 24:10 *And the servant took ten camels of the camels of his master and departed; for all the goods of his master were in his hand: and he arose, and went to Mesopotamia, unto the city of Nahor.*

Ten camels make a large caravan. And in today's world, we would view Abraham's camels as heavily guarded SUVs, accompanying our President. Today it would be a big motorcade followed by the media trying to get the scoop. Cameras would be everywhere.

I see one of those hidden messages here. To form a good marriage will take some effort. It's not what you see in those romantic comedies. It is true that two people can have a natural attraction to each other. Nevertheless, it can take time to make sure you know what the other person is all about. Successful things are not random accidents. They usually start with a vision. Steve Job's Apple Computer and iPhone were the result of a vision and a lot of effort to fulfill that vision. The dating process requires effort with eyes looking to the years to come. If you start out doing it God's way, you will have a greater chance of avoiding bad consequences.

The expected result from doing things God's way should be a lifetime of oneness with your soul-mate. Rebekah had no clue at this moment why the caravan had arrived, but in time she realized what was taking place was not a random event. Marriage was never intended by God to be an accident; it was always a result of planning and effort to prove all things. This doesn't fit with movie versions where romance spontaneously happens, and all are happy forever after. Dissatisfaction after a few years is why I am suggesting God's way.

Put some effort into dating by using God's methods. We will

continue finding them in the story. Ten black official-looking SUVs may not visit you, but you will be able to see God's involvement if you are looking with "spiritual eyes."

Think about all the effort being given to this process. Abraham could have found a local girl to make do. Of course, the thought of converting a young woman from her pagan religions never crossed his mind. Years later, in Rebekah's life, she sums up her thoughts about the local women from Canaan, saying they made her weary. Isaac and Rebekah's oldest son Esau had married two of them. One was a mistake; the second was a giant blunder. There is a reason Abraham was doing all this. As a Prophet, and as a man, he knew if you married trouble, you got in trouble. And Abraham should know if anybody would know.

Paul, in 1 Corinthians 6:14-17, tells us not to be unequally yoked. It's timeworn King James English; it means not to be mismatched. He is drawing our attention back to a picture from other stories in the Bible, where he is referring to men like himself as an ox, which is a powerful animal that can get the job done. The Old Testament example was trying to plow with an ox and a donkey together. These animals are unequally yoked in strength and attitude. These animals have different agendas. Some things just do not work well together, and this thought should be foremost in the dating process.

The message is simple: if you marry somebody who doesn't want God, you will live a life of insecurity with no trust. When you live with skepticism about your faith, you will often face disappointment. If you desire a relationship with your Creator but dwell with a person who does not want anything to do with God, you've got problems.

Did you notice that the name of the town is after Rebekah's family? The name Nahor is a subtle hint giving us information strongly suggesting she was not from a struggling family looking for a way out of her situation. Marriage is often to escape where a person is in life. But a bad marriage is still a bad marriage.

Rebekah seems to be very happy with her place in life. As the ten SUVs, I mean camels, turned up at the "well," this fantastic story starts to unfold. She immediately realized that she needed to pay attention. Something was taking place, and God was involved.

Our storyteller left out the long and challenging journey the caravan had in getting to the well. A journey to a good marriage will take some time, and the key activity is prayer. Abraham was undoubtedly home praying as Eliezer was suffering in the heat and the exhausting travel for several weeks.

I have been on a camel, and I didn't like it. Give me one of those black SUVs any day. There is no way I would want to spend several weeks on a camel unless it was of tremendous importance involving marriage for my children or grandchildren. I agree with Abraham. Everything had to be right. We are seeing God's plan for continuing the family line for the Seed of the woman. This family would be blessed because years later, God's Son Jesus would be delivered to live on earth by the great, many times great granddaughter of Abraham.

It should be the same for your marriage. You too are essential to God. He sent His Son to die so you could have eternal life. It is only a guess, but while you are here on earth, I think God desires you to have a good marriage as part of your salvation experience. A marriage done God's way does bring Him glory.

Seven

ARRIVAL AT THE WELL

Gen 24:11-20 *And he made his camels to kneel down without the city by a well of water at the time of the evening, even the time that women go out to draw water. And he said, O Lord God of my master Abraham, I pray thee, send me good speed this day, and shew kindness unto my master Abraham.*

Behold, I stand here by the well of water; and the daughters of the men of the city come out to draw water: And let it come to pass, that the damsel to whom I shall say, Let down thy pitcher, I pray thee,thatImaydrink;andshe shall say, Drink, and I will give thy camels drink also: let the same be she that thou hast appointed for thy servant Isaac; and thereby shall I know that thou hast shewed kindness unto my master.

And it came to pass, before he had done speaking, that, behold, Rebekah came out, who was born to Bethuel, son of Milcah, the wife of Nahor, Abraham's brother, with her pitcher upon her shoulder. And the damsel was very fair to look upon, a virgin, neither had any man known her: and she went down to the well, and filled her pitcher, and came up. And the servant ran to meet her, and said, Let me, I pray thee, drink a little water of thy pitcher.

And she said, Drink, my lord: and she hasted, and let down her pitcher upon her hand, and gave him drink. And when she had done giving him drink, she said, I will draw water for thy camels also, until they have done drinking.

And she hasted, and emptied her pitcher into the trough, and ran again unto the well to draw water, and drew for all his camels.

The storyline should immediately grab your attention. Look at the formal social protocol in play here.

> Gen 24:11 *And he made his camels to kneel down without the city by a well of water at the time of the evening, even the time that women go out to draw water.*

Eliezer had the camels kneel-down. This well did not belong to him. In the big picture of life on earth, God gives each of us what He wants us to manage. God is a God of details. When he gives us more than we need, as with this city well, the people who own it are to help those in need.

Eliezer was respectful of this principle. It's something crucial for Rebekah to see. It started her proving all things from the beginning. The first thing Rebekah sees is respect for others and their property. In the dating process, contempt for others and their property is a sign of what you should expect in the future.

Today, we would expect them to arrive with a cloud of dust in their black SUVs and grab the water hose as if it was their own. Why? Is it because we live in a society of entitlement? The modern mindset is, "I can take want I want because you have it, and I need it." We think of ourselves as our own "gods." It is the same thing we see in Satan's way of thinking, "God created it, I like it, and I will take it."

Water was and is still a big deal in the country of Israel. Digging a well was hard work, and not always successful. A working well was a prized possession. Eliezer set his caravan of camels down and waited for permission to water them. Eliezer was tracking with God. As soon as he arrived, he started praying. Did you notice his prayer? His concern was the mission. Here is another encoded clue to proper Biblical dating: prayer.

> Gen 24:12 *And he said, O Lord God of my master Abraham, I pray thee, send me good speed this day, and shew kindness unto my master Abraham.*

There are some prayerful things one should do before dating. Again, I remind you, dating is not just for fun. You marry people you date. I've included many suggestions that should be considered as we move through the story. Plus, there are a few ideas in the Appendix.

Here is one of them: Both the man and the woman should spend about the same time in spiritual preparation as they do physical. My guess is most ladies get the point here. Dating is important and time should be taken to be at your best. This usually happens naturally, but the hint is to add considerable time in prayer, preparing for spiritual understanding and wisdom. We see once again that God was involved, He is answering needs before requested. God does that often. They arrived at "evening time." They could have come earlier in the heat of the day, and the wait would have been long and hot. God is involved in this process and not only will Eliezer's crew and animals get water, but the expected difficulties in locating an available bride who meets all the requirements became apparent almost instantly.

The events of this story took years in the making. Like Eliezer's "travel time," to find your soul-mate will take conscientious effort. However, when God is working everything may line up suddenly, and become evident that God has been at work. Jesus told Abraham that an angel would go before them and we are now seeing what was prepared. But don't lose sight of the fact that "all things" still had to be proved.

God was in control and was moving this "search and locate" endeavor into the express lane. Eliezer was blessed with lightning fast speed and kindness. The result was that the team was led safely to the correct location at the right time. It was no accident; I suspect Eliezer was in continuous prayer from the time he left Abraham.

Gen 24:13 *Behold, I stand here by the well of water; and the daughters of the men of the city come out to draw water:*

Eliezer had done his part. They had arrived back to Abraham's family. He had covered the hot, dusty dry, boring miles, and positioned himself in the right place. Hint – encrypted code here, "positioned himself in the right place." He didn't go down to the local air-conditioned "beer-joint." He might have found some single women there, but not the one he was looking to find. We are about to see some amazing things about a girl named Rebekah. She is not the typical girl you would find at the "joint" down the road or walking around killing time at the local mall. If a man is looking for the right person to spend his life with, he should take a look at the things Rebekah was about to do. And if a young lady is seeking a soul-mate, Eliezer's actions (as Isaac's representative) are worthy of notice.

As for the caravan, the hard part was over, and the impossible part was about to start.

Eliezer was a wise man. He knew what to do. While we are looking at an arranged marriage procedure, the same elements must be used in "proper dating." Do what he did. Position yourself for success and present yourself as respectful of others. Then pray. It looks like a three-part process to me: position, presentation, and prayer.

Don't miss the last step, pray. Few people pray or even think about praying for one of the most critical steps in their life. It is part of the deception that dating is just for fun.

You might notice the particular request Eliezer is about to make in the next verse for a drink and watering the camels. Requirements like these will make certain that God is involved. What Eliezer asked for was not a probable series of events. They were possible, but not necessarily expected. Don't be silly here and add useless detail in your request to God. Pray for things that show you the type of person you are trying to find. For example, pray for normal everyday situations that show his or her integrity. I don't know that I had enough faith to pray like this when I was young. Nevertheless, I was looking for a young lady that was interested in the things of God. That was specific enough without bordering on the edge of requesting a minor miracle. In my own story of dating, I had an unusual mental idea of requirements if I was going to date. I was looking for a girl who wanted God in her life. I was not aggressively dating because I was preparing myself for a successful life. I wanted to be involved in the Lord's work but also wanted to be able to support a family if God led me into marriage. I knew that God would in time show me the person who had similar desires. And He did.

While dating, I knew very little about what God's Word said about marriage. I didn't have a handy-dandy short list of the biblical responsibilities of a husband or the list of the biblical responsibilities of a wife, having never heard of such a thing. The one I have now came from the years I spent as a youth pastor compiling information that came my way. I will share it with you.

The truth of the matter was simple. I was preparing myself for success and keeping my eyes open for my soul-mate. I didn't expect to find her anytime soon. I never made a written list. All I knew was that she would be a person who wanted God. I had no clue what I was expecting to see. Whatever it was, I saw it that day. In comparison to what Eliezer was looking for, my list seemed easy.

Eliezer's plan depended on God's answer. There is no chance his request could accidentally happen. And Rebekah's actions left no question about God's involvement. As you pray for spiritual insight, you are not testing God; your prayer should be for the understanding of what you see. You are looking for things that a believer seeking God would do. It could be a small, simple thing, but those who want God's leading will conduct themselves differently, just like Rebekah did by watering the camels.

Gen 24:14 *And let it come to pass, that the damsel to whom I shall say, Let down thy pitcher, I pray thee, that I may drink; and she shall say, Drink ,and I will give thy camels drink also: let the same be she that thou hast appointed for thy servant Isaac; and thereby shall I know that thou hast shewed kindness unto my master.*

Eliezer wants this bride candidate to volunteer to water ten camels, and that is no easy task. You might expect her to say, "Help yourself to some water for your camels." I would think that would be a satisfactory courtesy. But Eliezer wanted to be sure. His request would make it very evident that she was the one. When God is working, it's always clear. Eliezer believed that God had prepared a bride for Isaac. They were weeks apart in distance, but God had directed Abraham with wisdom on where to send Eliezer.

I had gone to the church college activity, not to find a wife, but to be around those who believed in God. The State University was not a very spiritual place. It was not a good idea to isolate myself from other believers. So, I attended church and activities as I could. Even though it was not my objective, I was in the right place to find a young woman who was seeking God. I did not have a "water-the-camel test," but I knew she was there for the same reason I was. She was headed to the State University herself, and her goal was not to find a husband, as she told me months after we started dating. She planned on getting a good education but knew she needed good Christian friends. We met at the well of Living Water.

Rebekah was just being herself that day, doing what was needed. She was not out looking for a husband but just living life correctly. She was merely taking care of the family.

On the handy-dandy list of marital responsibilities, one of them included for the wife is to be a help-meet. A help-meet is a helper who is "like" or suitable for him. Some one comparable to him. One translation says a "companion." Marriage is a partnership that works through life as it happens. God's plan takes two skill sets, of him and her, to provide and meet all the needs for getting through life – including children and forming a family. What we are about to see is God preparing a young woman who had the tools and personal motivation to be the wife of Abraham's son, Isaac.

Gen 24:15 *And it came to pass before he had done speaking, that, behold, Rebekah came out, who was born to Bethuel, son of Milcah, the wife of Nahor, Abraham's brother, with her pitcher upon her shoulder.*

Once again, we see some genealogy background. The meeting at the well was going to be a family thing. Rebekah came out of the house, out of the family to do her chores. And she had the credentials that Abraham has specified. She also had the right tool.

Interestingly, she had a pitcher on her shoulder. It doesn't seem to flow with the next verse very well. Verse sixteen tells us she is attractive. So, what is the deal with the pitcher? A water pitcher is not a piece of jewelry in any culture. Is God giving us a hint again? What do you think? Is this telling us she was prepared to do her job? Is this different than a "princess" on the porch waiting for her prince to arrive? I guess we will soon find out what makes Rebekah tick.

Rebekah's actions pre-qualified her as being an active part of a family. Life was hard in those days. Producing or finding food took a lot of time. Water didn't come out of a faucet in the kitchen. It had to be carried from the source. This daily task often went to the women and daughters as the men took on the harder work of farming. It appears to me what we are about to see is a young woman who understood and took her job seriously.

Gen 24:16 *And the damsel was very fair to look upon, a virgin, neither had any man known her: and she went down to the well, and filled her pitcher, and came up.*

We find what we would expect to see in the opening scene of a romance movie. The girl is always "very fair" or beautiful, and perhaps, stunningly beautiful. I know what you may be thinking. It's a good thing Isaac wasn't here, or this story would have been over. A movie script for Isaac would say, "She is the one," even before she ever said a word. And you know, in a movie today, Rebekah would have been cast as a beautiful woman by their definition of beauty. But what does "very fair" mean?

Beauty changes with culture. For example, in the 15th century beauty was different than what the movies tell us today. I looked up the Old Hebrew word in Strong's dictionary to see what "very fair" might mean. The definition and its root were mostly about "good." It seems to be quite different than what I thought it meant. Here are some of the ways the KJV translated "fair" in various places. The translation depended on context.

OT: 2896 KJV beautiful, best, better, bountiful, cheerful, at ease, fair, favors, fine, glad, good, graciously, joyful, kindly, kindness, loving, merry, most, pleasant, pleased, pleasure, precious, prosperity, ready, sweet, wealth, welfare, well-favored.

Did you get the impression that maybe beauty was not totally connected to sexual attraction as in a movie production? Beauty might be more about the characteristics of the person, not just what she was wearing or looked like? I get that feeling.

One thing I am sure about, Rebekah did not spend hours with the wardrobe and make-up department back home. She was dressed to carry water. No party dress here. And the Bible says she was beautiful.

In the story of Ruth, we see something about beauty. Many people like to say that Boaz was attracted to Ruth because of her physical beauty. But this is not in that story. It is how our blockbuster movie inspired imagination works. We must read these stories with spiritual eyes, instead of Hollywood sunglasses. The only thing Boaz seemed to notice was Ruth's faith in God and her treatment of Naomi. Ruth's faith was beautiful.

Beauty is more than skin deep. It is our brainwashed heads that change what God wrote. Rebekah, in her story, is beautiful, but not necessarily by our cultural definition. Her beauty was more than what meets the eye. And that is why this story is sixty-seven verses long. God is telling us things we cannot distort into something He did not mean. Marriage is not about appearance. "Beauty," in God's eyes, is something very different than the media world tells us.

Did you notice that Rebekah was living life God's way – not the world's way? It tells us twice she was a virgin. God wanted this point to be precise. She had maintained purity. Did you pick up on the encoding of truth here? God told it to us in two different ways to make sure we got it. God's plan is always purity. You might expect Satan's idea to be anti-purity - because it is.

If the Bible had background music, the score would pick up here in intensity.

Gen 24:17 *And the servant ran to meet her, and said, Let me, I pray thee, drink a little water of thy pitcher.*

The first institution God established was the family and how it should work. Will we see this with what Rebekah is about to do? Keep your eyes open as we move through the rest of this scene; see if you can pick up on the theme of family.

This scene wouldn't happen this way today. We know what young Rebekah would have done as this man ran towards her. She would have run away and called the police. Why did Eliezer run towards her? Was he excited, or in a hurry, as he played the "stand-in" role for Isaac? I think so. He jumps over the small talk and gets straight to the "water-the-camel test." As we watch, the question is, "What will she do?"

All young girls and boys today are trained to run from strangers. They are told to call for help in fear of an attempted kidnapping. Satan, and his World System, has used modern media to scare everybody from meeting an unknown person. (Particularly, if he is running towards you.)

This preconceived fear stops people from even meeting other people. It certainly stops God's people from telling God's story. If you try to be friends with complete strangers, they will be suspicious.

Rebekah did not turn and run. She felt safe, and I suspect a ten-camel caravan that is politely waiting for permission to get water had set her at ease. Evil minds do not take time to be polite and respectful – they just "take." (Encoded hint here – God gives, and evil takes what it wants.)

If ten black government vehicles pulled up while I was watering the yard, and they showed respect to my property, I would still want to know what was going on. With my television shaped imagination, I might still fear any man in a suit running toward me. It would make me think twice. But Rebekah hadn't seen the latest cop shows, and I suspect that Eliezer's running showed time was of value to his mission.

Eliezer spoke his request, and his heart must have been pounding with excitement. He could see the writing on the wall, or maybe I should say in the sand. God was about to do something astonishing, and Eliezer knew it. I would have run toward her myself, knowing I was about to see nothing short of a miracle. His old heart probably skipped a beat at her first words.

Gen 24:18 *And she said, Drink, my lord: and she hasted, and let down her pitcher upon her hand, and gave him drink.*

No doubt, he needed a drink. His travel has been in an unfriendly environment where water is rare. His thirst, however, was not the focus of this moment; the center of his attention was if God was answering prayers, or not.

Our heroine quickly jumps into action. She has the needed tool (a pitcher) to serve God's plan. And, she had already filled the pitcher. Notice the word "hasted." It could be the excitement of the arrival of such a prestigious party, and his running toward her to speak that caused her haste. Or it could just have been her nature. I vote for her nature as I hear the next words she speaks. Eliezer was probably ready to drop over dead with excitement. God, in just a few minutes, had answered his prayers of all these many weeks. God was saying, "Here is the one for Isaac." God often speaks through the actions of others, no words necessary. Eliezer knew what God was saying – "Here she is." As he took the drink, he was prepared to watch and see what was going to happen next.

Gen 24:19 *And when she had done giving him drink, she said, I will draw water for thy camels also, until they have done drinking.*

God left out the fireworks, parade, and applause. There is no hype or spin on the action. There is no close-up, or music to carry the story. We know, just like Eliezer, that God had prepared the way. If I had been there, I would have also been speechless. But the story is not over; it has just begun. Marriage involves three things, and we are only at step one.

The three components (body, soul, and spirit) in which God created men are about to surface in this story. I see a spiritual connection because Rebekah was not asked to do this. The spiritual connection is based on the truth. Eliezer needed a drink, and so did his ten beasts of burden. We do not know of any old custom that says she had to do this. We have no reason to believe this was expected social behavior. If it were customary, then Eliezer's prayer would be unnecessary. To us watching, this is unexpected. It's a little like her saying, "I will wash your ten SUVs because they are dusty." Who would do that?

Rebekah seems to have seen a need beyond normal. The undeniable truth was the camels needed water. You might suggest it was emotions that motivated her. But I think it would take a lot of love for camels to do what she did. Those who know say it could require at least twenty gallons of water each. Twenty gallons times ten is a lot of water to have enough. Rebekah did not give them a taste; she gave them "all" they needed.

How often do we give a token gift of effort instead of addressing the full situation of those in need? But Rebekah did. This tells us something special about her; she wants things done correctly, no matter the personal cost.

What Rebekah did was more than an emotional response to animals. I have been in a well in Israel. That's right; I was "in" the well. Our tour guide told me it was like the well in our story – perhaps it was so. In America, we are used to running springs, ponds, and other bodies of water for livestock. The climate in Israel is much different. They dug wells by hand. And these were not a 12" hole drilled down with a pump to move the water. Digging by hand meant the size was big enough for men to move up and down. The one I was in was several feet in diameter because it went down a long way and had steps along the inside walls that spiraled down. The stepped walkway down was narrow, and the steep steps were poorly formed. Not suited, in my eyes, to carry a pitcher of water up.

How big was the pitcher? Even if three gallons and if the well was not very deep, this was a monumental task. Most readers would see this as a literary exaggeration of what happened. But that is not how God works. The Word of God doesn't dramatize what is taking place. The Bible just tells us the facts and moves on to the next point. It may seem bizarre in our thoughts that anybody would give this much effort for a bunch of thirsty camels, particularly when the owners could do it.

But things were different in those days. My father walked several miles to school each day. Rain or snow. I walked a few blocks when I was in grade school. My children had to go all the way to the garage to ride to school. Nothing we experience is as hard as basic survival was in those days. Carrying water to the house for the family was Rebekah's job. You do what you must to stay alive. In our world today, most teens would reject the idea of serving a stranger and say, "You can water your own camels." Rebekah saw a need and willingly responded.

What we see with Rebekah's performance is more than you

would expect. Her motivation had to be more than the love of camels. It was a God-given reaction to those in need, including camels. And for me, camels would be on the bottom of the "I want to help list." They didn't use camels because they are cute and cuddly. Their value was in the fact that they could go a long distance without needing water. The relationship between camels and men is not a relationship of love. The camels would rather be elsewhere, and men would prefer an air-conditioned SUV. From what little I know, camels can be bad news and a lot of trouble. But, these ten camels needed water.

We are seeing a woman of character. She was not self-centered or lazy. Her motivation was meeting the needs of others. We are seeing that she faced a need and took care of it without being asked. And you must admit this was a monumental task. Rebekah kept working hard at the undertaking and finished. She had a servant's attitude, not an entitlement or "serve me" attitude. Are you adding to your list about how to prove all things? Rebekah's actions are more than Eliezer would expect. But they are what you might expect God to provide.

Gen 24:20 *And she hasted, and emptied her pitcher into the trough, and ran again unto the well to draw water, and drew for all his camels.*

She made good use of her time. She was always running and making haste. She didn't waste time trying to find an excuse for not watering the camels or for somebody to help her. It seems to me her focus was on the physical needs of these animals. Watering ten camels was hard, but their need was great. She did not say, "You do it." Not Rebekah. It was her job, and she did it – even if she did not have to.

In the family setting, it appears that it was Rebekah's place to keep water available for the family and she took this responsibility seriously, to the point of extending her duties to unknown visitors. Was her role performed because of integrity? Can you make a list of people you know who would do this kind of thing? If you try, it will probably only take a small piece of paper. But these people do exist. For example:

- Your parents, who gave up their dream for you.
- Your pastor, who sits up all night in the hospital with a sick church member.
- Teachers, who do more than they are paid to do.
- A person you might see as a soul-mate who is doing something because it is needed and for no other reason.

Bingo – another hint. Take note when you see God at work in somebody's life.

Eight

Could He Believe His Eyes?

Gen 24:21-22 *And the man wondering at her held his peace, to wit whether the Lord had made his journey prosperous or not.*

And it came to pass, as the camels had done drinking, that the man took a golden earring of half a shekel weight, and two bracelets for her hands of ten shekels weight of gold; And said, Whose daughter art thou? Tell me, I pray thee: is there room in thy father's house for us to lodge in?

And she said unto him, I am the daughter of Bethuel the son of Milcah, which she bare unto Nahor. She said moreover unto him, We have both straw and provender enough, and room to lodge in.

As Eliezer was assessing Rebekah's actions, it appears he remained speechless. What could he say?

Gen 24:21 *And the man wondering at her held his peace, to wit whether the Lord had made his journey prosperous or not.*

While Rebekah was responding to a physical need; she was doing so in the Spirit of the Lord. Eliezer was seeing God's Spirit at work in this young woman, and he knew by what he saw she was the right girl. I think this is another encoded message for developing correct dating principles. Here it is: Do things God's way (even if everyone else is not.) The ones who need to know will get the message God wants them to see.

Have you seen God at work? I have, and so did Eliezer. You can see God at work in a person's passion for doing a job right. What he saw was a girl who had a passion for good - for doing "good excellently."

Martha of the New Testament had that passion. It is a spiritual gift of the most exceptional kind until it interferes with what God is doing. Martha wanted Mary to have the same type of gift that she had. Unfortunately, her passion got in the way of Mary's hunger for sitting at the feet of Jesus and soaking in His words of truth.

We see the same thing happen to Rebekah with her son Jacob many years later. She knew whom God had chosen to carry on the bloodline of the Messiah, and her passion for doing "good" got in the way of what God was doing. But I am ahead of the full Bible story.

Eliezer, on this day, saw God at work, and so did Rebekah. The question posed in verse 24:21, as Eliezer watched to "know," was if God had made his journey prosperous or not. The focus was on what God was doing.

Some today see Jesus through tired eyes of people with a cold and dry Gospel. They have only seen a Gospel to make someone money, or to change behavior to what others would like to see. Doing right is seldom seen in our culture. And no doubt the shallow "I'll just get by" attitude also ruled in Eliezer's day. But here we all can see God at work. I believe Rebekah's watering effort was her godly nature doing what she loved to do. Everybody saw it. No questions here, the journey was prosperous.

At the office where I work, we refer to doing something for a demanding client beyond what they have paid, as being "Rebekah's" work because it is doing "good excellently." Doing things right is God's way of doing everything.

Have you ever seen somebody doing "good excellently" just because they could? No pay, no applause, no fame, just doing something because they could? Jesus did this with His miracles.

I think maybe that is why He made new wine in Canaan. He wasn't showing off; He was just doing "good excellently." God didn't have to send His Son to the Cross, but He did. It is an "excellent good" to forgive those who need forgiveness.

A godly marriage is an example of doing "good excellently." Two people in need of another, serving each other. Marriage is about giving and taking care of the one you have married. It is not about what you can take; it's about what you can give. Satan has destroyed this kind of thinking. Hollywood can't capture this kind of passion and sell it, so they use lust.

So, what is "lust"?

"Lust" is focusing on yourself, trying to get what you want. There is little regard for the consequences. Lust is about greed and control. You can think of it as selfishness, a contrast to love, which is about oneness and giving.

Lust is easier to sell. It is how fallen man is wired. The media incorporates "lust" into everything to generate physical desires in those watching. It is a win, win for Satan. However, when a couple lives as "one," meeting the needs of their soul-mate is all that matters. Movies need conflict to create interest. Marriage is about peace and movie makers would go broke if they tried to sell films based on a godly marriage. A godly marriage portrays "good" excellently done. Meeting the needs of a spouse is just part of daily life. It is not so easy to portray because it all happens so naturally for soul-mates. Their actions go unnoticed compared to the edgy drama of the modern media shock craze. It happens without fanfare. Practice looking for "good" excellently done. When you find it, you have found the person you need to discover, and if you are doing the same, they will find you.

> Gen 24:22 *And it came to pass, as the camels had done drinking, that the man took a golden earring of half a shekel weight, and two bracelets for her hands of ten shekels weight of gold;*

Did you notice the words, it came to pass? Rebekah's work was not a storybook exaggeration for effect – it happened, and it took a long time to water this many camels.

Back in verse 24:14, Eliezer had prayed a specific prayer that included an unexpected action from the girl he was searching to find. The prayer was for less than what Rebekah had done. Eliezer had prayed that she would provide the animals with water, but she gave them all they wanted. That is what it means when it says when they "had done drinking." These beasts would not quit until they had all they could hold and needed. This story is about ready to shift gears. We see Eliezer's prayer has found an answer.

What is about to happen with jewelry could be an emotional temptation. Keep your eyes open to see if the jewelry becomes Rebekah's motivation. Or will she continue to be driven by spiritual understanding and passion for helping those in need? To understand, we must dig deeper into the story. The Holy Spirit is very much involved in this historical event. Remember, Eliezer represents the Spirit of truth. He is the unnamed servant quietly overseeing this operation.

In the narrative, it is not Eliezer watching; it is the unnamed servant. Nowhere in the story are we told the name of this servant. We assume it is Eliezer, and we have no reason to believe otherwise. So why didn't God call Eliezer by name? Is it the encrypted code thing again? By leaving him unnamed, we can see him as a picture of the Holy Spirit.

This story is not just about Rebekah and Isaac. It is the story of "romance done right"—done God's way. By leaving the servant unnamed, Eliezer becomes unseen like the Holy Spirit. God's Spirit is unseen but indwelling in believers. Knowing about God's unconditional love, we might expect Him to be at work in making our life abundantly good even if we are not trying. Except for those given the gift to be single, God wants us to be married. For those given the gift to remain single and serve the Lord, we praise God. But as Paul said, for most, it is best that we not be alone (1 Cor 7:7 and see Appendix).

One of the concerns with marriages today is we have let our culture dictate who we marry. It should be the Indwelling Spirit of God doing the directing. What we need is the Spirit of Truth. When we trust God for His gift of Salvation, given to us through the sacrifice of Jesus on the cross, we are showing God that we believe in Him. We are saying we want God and His ways of righteousness. We want it done right.

Our acceptance of God's way is the opposite of Adam's and Eve's rejection of God when they took the forbidden fruit. Their actions proved they did not believe what God had said. Salvation through faith is saying we believe God's words. We are responding in a spirit of truth, by faith, to what He has told us.

In return, we receive The Holy Spirit. Jesus said in John 16:13, *"Howbeit when he, the Spirit of truth, is come, he will guide you into all truth..."* As we move through this story, I may refer to the Holy Spirit as the Spirit of Truth. That is enough for us to understand what is taking place. We know this invisible connection with God has resulted in oneness with all other Christians. We are all connected by The Holy Spirit of Truth. This spiritual connection is not to be broken by men as seen in Mark 10:9.

I am aware that some who read this might have gone through the tragedy of divorce. My wife and I have suffered with friends and family through this kind of struggle. I have no way of knowing what you have experienced. But I have seen the pain involved in divorce situations. My guess is you already know what God wants you to do. I will leave that up to the Holy Spirit of Truth.

Trying to save a marriage headed to divorce takes the same kind of thinking that we find in the story of Isaac and Rebekah. It must be done through God's eyes. Rebuilding marriages that have gone through the tragedy of divorce are much more difficult. And it is a fact of fallen life that some unions can never be put back together. What do you do then? The answer must be prayerfully thought out. Look for wise counsel. God will give you the correct answer. Only God can give you the peace and the right path to follow.

What if you are not born-again? If you are not a believer in Jesus Christ, I have a short section at the end called "What is meant by "Born-again?"" Marriage is not what you need to be concerned about if you have rejected God. Stop here and read - it is in the Appendix. For those who are born-again, you have the Indwelling Unseen Servant inside you. He will direct as you listen to His still small voice. Rebekah is looking at things through spiritual eyes. Meditate on what she does and says. Her reactions were not a result of glitzy jewelry.

So, what about all this flashy jewelry? What has golden earrings and massive bracelets to do with dating? Was it an emotional enticement to trick this young girl into marriage? If you use movie mentality, then you will miss what has just happened. Eliezer is acting in place of Isaac. He is doing what Isaac would do if he were there. The jewelry was not given to impress Rebekah - it has other purposes.

This unnamed servant already knows Rebekah is God's choice. It is now time to get all the rest of the people involved on board with what God is doing. These gifts of jewelry were not given to her as a way to thank her for the water. She knew the value of her work and that something "greater" is about to take place. Eliezer is redirecting the story to a new level. The expensive gifts to her personally established that something more is about to happen. Was it the proposal? But notice - Eliezer doesn't move forward with the proposal. Other things must first be proved. The Unnamed Servant is redirecting the story away from Rebekah to family - her family.

You see, family is the goal. "Family" is the result of a marriage, and in time it will produce other unions as the children grow up. God will not leave family out. It is part of the definition of marriage as we have already seen.

Gen 24:23 *And said, Whose daughter art thou? tell me; I pray thee: is there room in thy father's house for us to lodge in?*

Eliezer moves the conversation to the family. Without family as the authority structure, God's built-in process of life doesn't work well. Eliezer knew the procedure had to go through the right channels. And the process must include family. I might ask, "How can we expect a new family to function if it didn't function correctly in the original family?"

Before we get too far, we must discuss what happens if the family is out of the picture? The dysfunctional family is the norm these days. But being dysfunctional is not an excuse to cut them out of the process. Ex 20:12 *"Honour thy father and thy mother: that thy days may be long upon the land which the Lord thy God giveth thee"* is not a suggestion. It is one of the Ten Commandments. And in this story, we will see all the family involved. As we continue, we will discover hidden in this story roots of a dysfunctional family.

There are many situations where parents on one or both sides of a future marriage will reject God's involvement. I was married in an era where Christians were well respected, but now after decades of abuse at the hands of the media, many think believing in God is a silly choice. Like I said, "The Lie" has become very powerful. Those who reject Jesus know the world is a mess. And they think their false god is going to fix it. It's a nice dream but void of any truth. The next release of a new cell phone or video game is not going to change the course of history. The result of the media's mishandling of families, as God had designed them, is dying families. Men cannot fix this mess. Only God can fix it.

So, how do you live in a country full of dysfunctional families? Speak the truth. Show those who ignore God what He is doing in your life. We must honor our parents, but parents did not create the institution of marriage— God did. Use your God-centered dating experiences as a testimony to the Truth of God. Respect your parents, but obey God.

Satan's attacks have been continuous against the family. God's plan has always been family centered around Him. As "family" is being destroyed, the picture God has painted for us becomes abstract and seemingly useless. The family today is almost always left out of the marriage process, especially the dating part. I wonder if there is a connection here with the fact dating doesn't work very well in many cases.

Watch what is about to happen as Eliezer, the unseen servant, moves through some challenging situations to bring about a godly marriage between two people who trust God.

We know from verse 24:15 that Rebekah is a daughter living in a town named after her family. But Eliezer did not necessarily know about the financial status of Rebekah's family, so he politely asks if there was room for his large procession of people and animals. Eliezer knew he had the right girl but was she from the right family? What better way than to ask if there is a place for him to stay so he might learn what he needs to know?

Gen 24:24 *And she said unto him; I am the daughter of Bethuel, the son of Milcah, which she bare unto Nahor.*

Here we see she understood family. And she was proud to tell about her ancestors. The name of the town was Nahor the name of Abraham's brother. That is the way they did it back in the day. A father would produce a family that would build a city that would create a nation. That is what Abraham's covenant with God said. And we are about to see that Rebekah is going to be added to this Covenant Plan.

The first place we see Abraham's unique relationship to God is in Genesis Chapter 12. We know Abraham is told to leave his idolatrous home and make a new life in an unknown "Promised Land." God wanted Abraham and his descendants to produce the coming Messiah and take the Good News to all the earth. Isaac's wife was the next significant step forward.

Gen 24:25 *She said moreover unto him; We have both straw and provender enough, and room to lodge in.*

The family was financially stable, and she knew it. She was well provided for and was not struggling or looking for a way out of town. And we are about to see she was a woman of great integrity. She knew the value of the jewelry, but she was all about family, so she did not let it turn her head. She was ready for the next step. Remember, no one in Rebekah's family knows the purpose of Eliezer's mission. His companions may have known something, but we do not know if they heard Eliezer's prayer. Rebekah certainly had no clue, but the impressive gifts changed everything. The situation has now become important for Rebekah, whatever the objective.

Please note, she did not invite them to stay; she just answered his question. It was not her place to welcome guests into the home. Nevertheless, Eliezer had seen enough. Without knowing what was going to happen in the hours to come, he already knew that God was at work, and he reacted to what he had seen. Don't minimize this next verse. When we see God at work, we should have the appropriate response. How many times has God answered prayer, and we moved on as if nothing had happened?

Nine

The Correct Response

Gen 24:26-32 *And the man bowed down his head, and worshipped the Lord. And he said, Blessed be the Lord God of my master Abraham, who hath not left destitute my master of his mercy and his truth: I being in the way, the Lord led me to the house of my master's brethren.*

And the damsel ran, and told them of her mother's house these things. And Rebekah had a brother, and his name was Laban: and Laban ran out unto the man, unto the well.

And it came to pass, when he saw the earring and bracelets upon his sister's hands, and when he heard the words of Rebekah his sister, saying, Thus spake the man unto me; that he came unto the man; and, behold, he stood by the camels at the well.

And he said, Come in, thou blessed of the Lord; wherefore standest thou without? for I have prepared the house, and room for the camels. And the man came into the house: and he ungirded his camels, and gave straw and provender for the camels, and water to wash his feet, and the men's feet that were with him.

There was much to be thankful for on this day. Abraham was getting old, and his son Isaac was not married. Isaac was the next patriarch in the lineage of The Messiah. So, Abraham sent an unidentified servant to find a wife for his son. Can you imagine the difficulty in this task? Leaving your home and going far away to find the perfect soul-mate for another person would be tough. It would be difficult doing this for yourself, but what if it was for the Boss's son? My thought on the matter is that it would be impossible - unless God is going to provide the answer.

Gen 24:26 *And the man bowed down his head and worshipped the Lord.*

This unnamed servant ended up in the right place, at the right time, to see the right girl, do the right thing. I believe he had every reason to be overcome with worship.

The joy of being in a place where God is working is hard to describe. To see your faith proved in the life of other people is nothing short of extraordinary. To watch God as He answers prayer will leave you on a spiritual high for days. But on this day God outdid Himself. With years of preparation, God had secured the perfect wife for Isaac. What Eliezer and the camel drivers experienced was beyond words. Worship happened.

It is the story of marriage - oneness is the right way to be in the image and likeness of God. One man, one woman, and one God are the three necessary parts. This oneness creates a desire for a couple to do "good" to the best of their abilities. Unity will produce a stable marriage. It is a oneness of purpose, and it is good. And I might ask, do those trying Satan's method of lust find lasting joy in marriage? When little effort is made, excellent results cannot be expected.

It is in this story that I eventually found what I experienced fifty years ago. It explains why I have said, "I want to be married." That is the result when marriage is done God's way. Marriage must involve the Spirit of God.

We are now seeing some of the secret ways of producing a good marriage. They were hiding in plain sight. We will soon see the secret ingredient is God's Spirit. Eliezer saw God at work, he knew it, and Eliezer worshiped.

Worship is a word that gets a lot of abuse today. It sometimes gets turned into little more than a "music concert" on Sunday morning. Don't take this wrong, a concert can turn into worship, but does not hold this title until it does. It is only worship if it is transferring worth to God.

In a different story, one about Abraham and Isaac, we see for the first time, this word "worship" in the Bible. God tested Abraham's faith by asking him to sacrifice his son Isaac. Yes, it's the same son that will marry Rebekah. Abraham did not understand it all, but he believed God and did as told in Genesis 22:5-14. Isaac was never in danger of death by being sacrificed. God doesn't work that way. But Abraham's faith was genuine worship. Abraham's faith transferred great value to God because he believed God and obeyed.

God wants us to believe, trust, and obey what He says. He's looking for people who desire Him for who He is – our Creator and Provider.

On this day, Eliezer and all the rest saw God at work through the young girl, Rebekah, whom God had prepared to become the matriarch of the Chosen Family – the family that would produce the Messiah. Sarah was dead, Rebekah was young, and God was moving on with His plan by providing a bride for Isaac. This day has resulted in authentic worship. Lives changed because of what God was doing. That is what worship should be, changed life. So, Eliezer prayed these words:

Gen 24:27 *And he said, Blessed, be the Lord God of my master Abraham, who hath not left destitute my master of his mercy and his truth: I being in the way, the Lord led me to the house of my master's brethren.*

His worship was for God's faithfulness in doing the impossible, so all would know what was happening. God should be seen so clearly in the dating and marriage process that those involved want to worship and praise God for what He is doing. I think I just wrote something important; did you get it?

Abraham had a long relationship with God, and his servant Eliezer had seen a lot of stuff during all these years. This day he saw God honor Abraham by keeping the covenant promise alive. It had taken years, but God is never late. And when the time was right, it was all going to take place quickly.

For the first time, Rebekah got a hint that the day's activities were part of an undertaking from God. Her behavior was impeccable before she knew what was taking place; she did not have to change the way she acted for anybody. What we have seen is who she is.

Now the story is changing for her also. What started as ten needy camels are turning into a "God thing." Her actions show us that she knew a little about God and His ways. Excitement about what was taking place is starting to energize a girl who is always motivated.

Gen 24:28 *And the damsel ran and told them of her mother's house these things.*

Do you get the impression this day was becoming significant to Rebekah? I believe it was full speed ahead. She ran, or maybe it was a sprint. My guess is most track coaches would have been proud of her time. She had a mission, and it wasn't about what she had done. As the story unfolds, we know it wasn't just about her actions. For Eliezer, it was about what she had said. He was hunting for a specific girl. Had he found her? He continued to move forward with the next step and gave her incredible gifts of gold. Proof enough that he wasn't running a scam.

Dating today can often be a game of fraud. Most people can put on a good act for a short time. They use "big talk" to impress, or whatever it takes to deceive another to get what they want. That doesn't mean that gifts aren't given to add to the discussion. But not jewelry like this. Some say these gifts of jewelry were about the same as a year's wages. He gave them with no strings attached. Did you notice the story never says she told others about the jewelry? I know they could see it, but her focus seems to be on Eliezer and his worship to God. These gifts gave her evidence that God was involved in all this. They came from a man who prayed and gave thanks to God for what had happened. Gold is nice, but God's involvement in your life is on a totally different level. I think Rebekah could see this and it was her primary motivation.

"The Lie" that dating is only for fun thrives on a fantasy approach. But marriage is real, and all the events before, during, and after should be weighed against and compared to what a soul-mate will be in years to come. Insecurity at the dating level is easy to spot if you get over the emotional rush of gifts. When God is out of the picture – emotions can easily override the spirit of truth. I believe that for Rebekah, her real excitement was for the involvement of God, even over the expensive jewelry.

Eliezer had seen enough, and Rebekah sprinted back home. Her running added to the evidence for Eliezer. Rebekah knew this was real; whatever was going to take place. The gifts were evidence that proved his prayer, and his worship was authentic. Can you feel the excitement about what God was doing as she told the family the high points of her experience?

Gen 24:29 *And Rebekah had a brother, and his name was Laban: and Laban ran out unto the man, unto the well.*

We also see Rebekah had a proper relationship with her family. Time always becomes valuable in extreme situations. The caravan had turned this average day into something extraordinary. Inviting them to stay was not Rebekah's position in the family. It was time for her father to take over. But he doesn't enter the story here.

Maybe the Father wasn't home when she arrived, and her brother stepped up to bat. It is evident that whatever was taking place could not wait, so it appears the son filled in for his dad.

God was doing something, and it was taking place at the "well." We hear the words she told her brother, who was apparently the oldest man present at the house. He immediately saw the significance and moved to fill the gap.

Notice that Laban saw the jewelry – nowhere in the story does Rebekah speak of the jewelry.

> Gen 24:30 *And it came to pass when he saw the earring and bracelets upon his sister's hands, and when he heard the words of Rebekah his sister, saying, Thus spake the man unto me; that he came unto the man; and, behold, he stood by the camels at the well.*

The gifts of jewelry reappear in the story. I believe that these items were not about watering the camels nor payment for the water. Rebekah seemed to understand, but I'm not so sure about Laban. Did he see this as an opportunity to get rich quick? It is not in this story, but years later we can see he willfully deceived Jacob in a marriage situation with his daughters.

The gold jewelry must have caught his eyes; it was supposed to. But it was the words Rebekah spoke that should have been his motivation, not the glitz. We will soon find other reasons to question Laban, but for now, he has moved himself to the "well" after making some preparations and found Eliezer.

This was not a poor family, and I do not believe it was expensive jewelry that was the incentive for their actions. But the gift did prove this was a serious encounter. People do not give costly gifts without reason. The text provides us with concern. It specifically says, Laban "saw" the jewelry.

Go back and re-read the words Eliezer spoke after giving gifts. His focus was on spending more time, not with her, but her family. The family is the theme of the last few and the following verses. Again, the encoded secret is that dating, and marriage are about family and proper relationship. When God isworking and placing two souls into a lifelong marriage, it will not be about some gift, even an expensive one. The focus should rapidly move to what God is doing and His involvement in bringing two people together. And in this story, it does. When you are dating God's way, proper behavior and the topic of conversation become clues to the future. What you see is what you get.

> Gen 24:31 *And he said, Come in, thou blessed of the Lord; wherefore standest thou without? for I have prepared the house, and room for the camels.*

It is obvious; Laban saw that God blessed Eliezer. My question is, did Laban put God in the story here to give the impression of understanding, or did he truly understand? Before he ran to the well, he set into motion the necessary preparations for the men that God had sent. Was Laban star struck about the caravan, gold jewelry or the thought of money? Perhaps. But he had picked up the proper theme from his sister. Listen to his words, "*Come in, thou blessed of the Lord; wherefore standest thou without.*" These words tell us that this is a God thing - a spiritual power play.

I may be putting Laban is a negative light. I do this not because of the things he does now, but things he will do later in this story and in future years in other Bible stories. I see him as an opportunist always ready to run a scam. Watch out for this kind of person and the advice they give. Use discernment with those who are "capable" of scheming and defrauding at your expense. One thing for sure, Laban knew this situation needed to move inside. Perhaps it was hospitality for what God was doing, or maybe he just wanted to see what he might gain personally. Again, Laban's trustworthiness is questionable to me. However, this doesn't mean he wasn't responding to what God was doing correctly. When God is working, even those who don't always involve God can see what is happening and respond. This is a huge point here. When God is working, everything will unfold - just like God planned. We have a Bible full of this truth.

Gen 24:32 And the man came into the house: and he ungirded his camels, and gave straw and provender for the camels, and water to wash his feet, and the men's feet that were with him.

This verse may be confusing as to who took care of the camels. The phrase "his camels" leads me to think this was Eliezer. The phrase "the men's feet that were with him" could mean Eliezer or Laban. Most translations seem to maintain this pattern. However, some commentaries state that it was Laban who did this. This would seem logical in view of what Rebekah had just done. But it doesn't fit in the later characteristics of Laban in the Bible.

Because it says, "his camels," I tend to think Eliezer oversaw this work, so I will make the following observations. These observations are true even if it was Laban, but I struggle with the interpretation that it was Laban doing the work. I am sure Laban made the supplies available, but Eliezer appears to be very involved.

One would think this list of details was not necessary to the story, but it is in the details where the truth becomes known. Eliezer was a man after God's ways, doing what was needed even if there were more exciting things to do. Eliezer could have left this to one of the other men. But a man of integrity does not do this. Eliezer is only a servant, but a servant takes his cues from his master. I suspect this list of chores that Eliezer took care of personally spoke volumes to Rebekah and her family.

She could see that Eliezer was no fraud. A person with no concern for looking after his animals' well-being is a person you do not want to date. It is one of the things you look for while dating. A modern-day example might be how the person you are with reacts to excellent service at a restaurant. Are they thankful and show appreciation in some way, perhaps a tip – or is it ignored? There are lots of reasons this may mean nothing, but it is a warning sign that something may be wrong if appreciation is never shown for what others do for you. It is also a flag down on the play if a person doesn't take care of the things in which he is in charge. Personal integrity is shown in the details of everyday life.

There is a test I believe we should not ignore. If your date uses a ten-dollar bill to pay for something, and the person at the cash register gives him change for a twenty, does he quickly pocket or bring it to the attention of the cashier? If somebody cheats a worker out of ten bucks, he will cheat anybody for what he can get – and that includes you.

The washing of feet is something we don't understand today. But back in those days, it was a significant need. It had to do with comfort, I would think. The point we should see is it says, Eliezer's feet "and" the men's feet. He made sure these men had the same level of comfort.

These are many things that Rebekah should have been looking to see on this day. If this unnamed servant had neglected his men and work animals, then this would have had a reflection on Isaac. A servant like Eliezer was a trusted family member; what he did away from Isaac's family is a good indication of how the family functioned. Here is one of those encrypted points showing why the family should be involved. The old saying, "The nut doesn't fall far from the tree," has merit. Don't get me wrong, you cannot always transfer what the family does to the one you are dating, but if you see significant issues, keep your eyes open for similar tendencies. Many people of great integrity have roots in lousy family experiences. Their bad experience could possibly be the catalyst to a righteous life. However, there was a reason Abraham did not want Isaac to marry a local girl from Canaan. He knew bad family traits could pass to the children and to future generations.

Ten

Time to Eat—Not Yet

Gen 24:33-41 *And there was set meat before him to eat: but he said, I will not eat, until I have told mine errand. And he said, Speak on.*

And he said, I am Abraham's servant. And the Lord hath blessed my master greatly; and he is become great: and he hath given him flocks, and herds, and silver, and gold, and menservants, and maidservants, and camels, and asses. And Sarah my master's wife bare a son to my master when she was old: and unto him hath he given all that he hath.

And my master made me swear, saying, Thou shalt not take a wife to my son of the daughters of the Canaanites, in whose land I dwell: But thou shalt go unto my father's house, and to my kindred, and take a wife unto my son.

And I said unto my master, Peradventure the woman will not follow me.

And he said unto me, The Lord, before whom I walk, will send his angel with thee, and prosper thy way; and thou shalt take a wife for my son of my kindred, and of my father's house: Then shalt thou be clear from this my oath, when thou comest to my kindred; and if they give not thee one, thou shalt be clear from my oath.

And I came this day unto the well, and said, O Lord God of my master Abraham, if now thou do prosper my way which I go;

It is easy to see that everyone would be hungry by this time. You get water from a well during the cool parts of the day.

Work time was over, and it was time to refuel. With the food in place, the body would start to react. And you know when you are hungry you want to eat. By all rights, the discussion that was about to happen could have waited. That would have been my vote. But not so for Eliezer. He was on a mission from God. And God's purpose was to come first. Somehow, God's angel had been at work in Rebekah's home in the city named after her grandfather Nahor.

Gen 24:33 *And there was set meat before him to eat: but he said, I will not eat until I have told mine errand. And he said, Speak on.*

Rebekah's family has been witnessing this from the very beginning. They know this is no ordinary discussion about to take place. To hear what Eliezer had to say preempted the need to eat. You can see the Spirit of Truth was in control of the physical and emotional desires of all the people involved.

I see this as a God-given test to see what her family would do. Their response was good news and served as a good example of how God's Spirit works. Dating and marriage create a lifelong relationship. Don't rush something important for a meal that can be delayed. A decision for a lifetime must take priority. Snap decisions have ruined more lives than can be counted. And the collateral damage may not be known for years.

The matter at hand was "considered" to be important by all. The meal could wait, and it did.

Gen 24:34 *And he said I am Abraham's servant.*

Here we have an introduction. Eliezer was a servant of a man they knew. Nahor's brother, Abraham, moved years ago, and we do not know how much communication existed between them. There was at least limited communication because we know that Abraham had heard that Nahor's son, Bethuel had an unmarried daughter named Rebekah (Genesis 22:20-24.)

Because idolatry existed at that time in history, with many believing in idols of wood and stone, it would be unheard of for someone to leave their family behind to travel to an unknown land because God told them to go. But that is what happened to Abraham. Abraham had talked to God, and Rebekah's family knew this story from years ago. As they now listened to Abraham's servant, Eliezer, much was to be considered.

Abraham's level of belief was astounding, and faith like this should be respected. We have a lot of material about Abraham which contains an excellent record of his character. It seems Abraham's family has some level of belief in His God. And this was Abraham's servant now standing before them. They gave him due respect.

It is here that the physical gifts of gold jewelry became proof. The golden gifts showed that Nahor's brother is blessed by great wealth. Just as God had told Abraham, he had told his family. Everything was making sense. But to make sure, Eliezer wanted the family to know what had happened to their great-uncle over the last few years.

Physical and spiritual history says a lot about family. God's gift of salvation is for everyone. The past doesn't have to go deep, but in this story, God wanted a young lady who had strong roots of integrity to fill the shoes of Sarah. Isaac's new bride would be stepping directly into the matriarchal position as family leader. There was no place for failure in the days to come.

Life is short for humanity on earth today. Seventy years is not very long. There is no time to waste on experimental or alternate and substitute replacements for marriage. The baggage picked up by mistakes in dating and marriage stay with you even if you start over. Take your time in the dating process; play it God's way. It takes a lot less time than starting over and living with memories of the past. Examine the spiritual side of your date. It is a big part of this story for a reason. Failure happens so often today because deception is not perceived during the dating process. Without acknowledging "The Lie," your chances are significantly reduced in forming a lasting and good marriage.

It is about time for Rebekah and her family to understand the spiritual side of this event. They have heard what Rebekah has told them, but they needed it first hand, and who better than Eliezer to tell them. As the servant in our story remains unnamed, the Spirit of God also remains unseen. Nevertheless, like the wind, we can see the physical things God's Spirit has done.

Gen 24:35 *And the Lord hath blessed my master greatly, and he becomes great: and he hath given him flocks, and herds, and silver, and gold, and menservants, and maidservants, and camels, and asses.*

His first words were words of praise for what has happened in Abraham's life of obedience and faith. If anybody knew what God had done, it would be Eliezer. Rebekah's family has already seen the gold jewelry and the ten camels, but what does it mean to say the Lord has blessed. There are several things mentioned here. The first is important.

Abraham has become great in social standing, because of his relationship with God. The things noted in verse 24:35 are not very important if Abraham had obtained them unfairly or keeps them selfishly close. If a man is always taking, and never giving, we should question the man's greatness. Taking is not a proper way to accumulate wealth. God blessed Abraham, and the result is a different kind of wealth.

We can see the kind of man Abraham is by the rescue of his nephew Lot years earlier. Abraham risked everything to rescue him. Lot had been taken captive by warring kings who overtook several smaller kingdoms. Abraham had trained men, 318 to be exact, and he rescued his nephew. He then gave a tithe to Melchizedek, King of Salem; this speaks volumes about Abraham. Then Abraham refused to take anything from the king of Sodom as pay for his valiant effort. He gave it all back.

So, we see Abraham was a great man. He had flocks and herds, which means he had more than just sheep. Silver shows he had wealth to spare to give an expensive gift as he wished. He had camels and donkeys. These were work animals used in the work of transportation for trading. He was not just a farmer with some animals – he was a businessman. He had true wealth. Yes, Abraham was great.

The family needed to know that Rebekah would be part of an established family, one that was blessed by God. We can see the spiritual, physical, and emotional side of this information all in one sentence.

In the dating world, we should NOT be looking for wealth and financial prosperity. Stuff like this is often lost in a heartbeat. What we should be looking for is a great blessing from God. It may not be money, but it will be evident in the spiritual connection that God is providing and protecting. This spiritual blessing is the source of real joy, even if we do not acquire many possessions. What we must have is God involved in our lives. That is greatness; everything else is just extra.

Gen 24:36 *And Sarah my master's wife bare a son to my master when she was old: and unto him hath he given all that he hath.*

In one short statement, Eliezer spoke the results of years of time. His first words seemed impossible. When Sarah was old, she gave birth to a son. You could say it was a miraculous birth.

This miraculous birth is another encrypted code in plain sight. All of God's stories have extended meanings. They pre-picture what God is going to do. It was in the rescue plan of humanity - if Adam and Eve rejected God.

Sarah giving birth at her age was miraculous and pre-pictured the virgin birth of Jesus. Isaac's birth was not a virgin birth, just a seemingly impossible birth. The concept here is that Isaac is a type of Jesus Christ. That would mean that Rebekah would pre-picture, the Bride of Christ. You should be able to see many similarities, such as the high price to be paid for the bride and the work of the Holy Spirit as the unseen servant. They all point to the Church. This story, within a story, amplifies the requirement for the Bride to be of great integrity.

All marriages pre-picture the marriage of Jesus to His Bride the Church, even yours. This is a big hint. If marriage pictures the relationship between Jesus and the Church, some of the statements I make should become vibrant and more meaningful. Marriage is important to God because it pictures the marriage of His Son.

While this is a beautiful thought for born-again believers, Rebekah's family also got the point. Isaac was Abraham's son, and Isaac would have an inheritance. Verse 24:36 answers many questions Rebekah's family might have had. The bottom line was evident. Rebekah would be well provided for and protected. At this point, marriage had not yet been mentioned, but I suspect the entire family knew what was about to be said.

Gen 24:37 *And my master made me swear, saying, Thou shalt not take a wife to my son of the daughters of the Canaanites, in whose land I dwell:*

The topic of marriage now enters the discussion. With a few sentences, Eliezer had cleared up many questions about Abraham. Rebekah's family needed to hear this. The Canaanites had adopted the practice of sacrificing their children to their false gods. Even though there was no television, Internet, magazines or newspaper, the Canaanites' reputation had preceded them, even in Mesopotamia, hundreds of miles away.

The Canaanites' "gods" of wood and stone are a little hard to comprehend in our culture. But what was going on is easy to see. It was all "made-up" lies spoken by the false priests who owned the carved images. These "priests" told the Canaanites how to make their do-nothing-gods happy. By doing this, the people thought they could control and manipulate these fake gods into helping them with things like weather, for instance.

This scam was profitable to the fake priest that managed them. The people's unjustified faith was out of control to the point they would sacrifice their children to appease these false gods. It's a lie straight from hell if I ever heard one. We can be sure that these people were known everywhere for this extreme practice. The unnamed servant had just explained not only a physical reason but a spiritual reason why Isaac could not marry into the Canaanite culture in which he lived. Eliezer also showed that Abraham had rejected this false religion as they would have expected. Before the family even had time to form questions, they had answers.

Are you starting to see what dating is about? It is a time to discover answers to your unasked questions. The family is a starting point. What you need to know will become evident as you date. In our dysfunctional world, a family may be out of the picture. But the same procedure applies. What you see and hear may not be from family - it may be from friends. Things you learn before a date can tell you what you might need to know during a date or perhaps, you realize it is not going to be a relationship you should pursue because a person is not spiritually controlled by God.

Where someone wants to go on a date can tell you who they are. Is a movie with a bad rating a good sign? What time of day and for how long? Is this a solo date or a date with other people? Think about it. What would you consider to be a proper place to get to know somebody? Is that what you want? If it doesn't sound right, it is not right.

If you are desperate to date for fun, and that is all you want, you are on your way to disaster. Analyzing all aspects of something to find answers to questions you have not asked can slow down an emotional rush into a relationship. Especially one based on lust. A spiritual investigation should be ongoing, even during a simple date to get ice cream.

Take as long as you need. If we read between the lines, with God involved, we can see what we need to know before we make critical decisions. Rebekah had all the major questions answered and proof of sincerity before she even knew what was going on. So should you.

Gen 24:38 *But thou shalt go unto my father's house, and to my kindred, and take a wife unto my son.*

The more significant part of the story peeks through the narrative here. The Messiah, the Seed of the woman, must be delivered into the world in an extraordinary and predicted way. The bloodline was everything. Isaac, as the father, could have been enough, but at this time, God wanted it to be as pure as possible. There are many variations in the years to come. There are even four brides in the bloodline of the Messiah that are of Gentile descent. Each has an extraordinary, spiritual story. But this is only the second generation, and the rejection of God by His chosen people was years away.

Numerous people believe God has prepared a special soul-mate just for each of us who desire marriage. I like this idea and think it has great merit. However, I cannot show you this in the Bible, but it would not surprise me at all if God has made someone just for you. I get a sad feeling about this approach. What if somebody was made to be your soul-mate and was being held captivated by deception, and you could not identify them. Or what if you have taken the wrong path to marriage and they cannot find you?

We can be sure if God has a soul-mate especially for us, it will become apparent. We have no way of knowing how God is going to bring two people together. Unless we are prayerfully filtering everything through spiritual eyes, we could miss it. This is where I get that sad feeling. However, I believe in a powerful God. I believe He cannot fail. I believe He will always succeed.

Some may never accept or realize what God has done for them. That doesn't change God's working in their lives.

Some may think God is not involved in the marriage process. Nevertheless, the same approach still works. By sifting all things through a spiritual filter, a person can be found who will become a faithful and trustworthy soul-mate. We do not have to know how God is working in our lives, but He is.

So, what is the point of these last few paragraphs? It was stated twice—using spiritual insight will always lead us in the right direction. Daniel purposed in his heart not to defile himself with the king's meat. He stayed faithful to what little he knew about God and the ways of God. If we are old enough to date, we are old enough to read God's Written Word. That is how the Spirit of God works. God's Spirit will move our minds back to the truth we read in the Bible to help throughout each day. What is read each morning will most likely be needed some time that day. But we must look for it.

The Bible is a love letter to the Bride of Christ. He left it for us, so we could know. Again, if you struggle with the old King James, get a more contemporary version. The Words of God should be exciting to you unless your focus is being held enslaved by the glitz of the world. But that is the plan of "The Lie," that we find the Bible irrelevant. If you are not a believer, take the time to investigate what this means.

Abraham knew about Rebekah even before he sent Eliezer. And his servant knew from years of being around Abraham what righteousness was. Eliezer's nature was to do what was right. He also could tell that Rebekah and the entire family were aware God was involved.

Gen 24:39 *And I said unto my master, Peradventure the woman will not follow me.*

We first saw this way of release from the oath made by Eliezer in case the woman would not come back with him. The mission was not an easy one; it could quickly fail. In a good relationship, you do not make unreasonable demands. I see the connection between Abraham and Eliezer to be one of mutual respect. Eliezer felt the freedom to ask what he should do if the woman would not come, and Abraham gave a release from the oath. Abraham did not expect a man to do what only God can do. Oh, I think I just dropped that hint again.

Men with great wealth and power like Abraham can become a dictator and make unreasonable demands with consequences. That is not God's way, and Abraham was God's man. We do not know much history between Abraham and Eliezer but, what we do know, it was not one of domination as was experienced with slavery in America years ago.

This position of Eliezer as a servant seems to be by choice. Eliezer is not a slave in a relationship of oppression as we had before the Civil War in this country. It was more of a position where the servant is like family. The servant's personal needs were open to discussion and considered important. Men who have wealth need help to run their estates. They seek people who need homes and a job. The slave/servant relationship is better defined in the years to come by the Old Testament Law as seen in Lev 25:25, 39.

Don't be surprised at how God works. The release from the oath had another significant revelation in this story. The release meant one thing to Eliezer, and something entirely different to Rebekah. This "release" part of the story informed Rebekah that she had a "say" in what was happening. Take note, the freedom of choice was in place before any proposal for marriage. She had the right to say yes or no. God has always given humanity free choice, even though he knows we often make bad decisions. Unconditional love demands free choice so love can function. We see this clearly with Eliezer's release from the oath statement. It is necessary for everybody to understand this because of a question they will ask Rebekah later.

> Gen 24:40 *And he said unto me, The Lord before whom I walk, will send his angel with thee, and prosper thy way; and thou shalt take a wife for my son of my kindred, and of my father's house:*

Abraham's answer to Eliezer changes the focus of the mission from Isaac needing a wife, to God's involvement in providing the perfect wife. God's actions in the story were now considered to be significant. Neither Nahor nor Abraham's family had a clear understanding of what the "Seed" of Abraham was to do. Notice I said "seed" as singular not seeds. The purpose of Abraham's children was to establish a family that would provide a platform through which Jesus could come and dwell with men. It all started in Genesis Chapter Twelve and ended in Matthew Chapter One. It is the story of a struggle this family had for centuries that fills these many pages. After the Cross, we can look back and see how it all worked, but they could not see this clearly. And neither did Satan.

As we read the reaction to the next few verses, it is evident that both families had some understanding of God's involvement. It is apparent that Abraham had a close relationship with the Lord because of what he said. Abraham was told God was going to send an angel ahead, and He did.

Many unexpected things have happened since the caravan's arrival at the well. The angel had completed his work. And now Nahor's family knows why: "thou shalt take a wife for my son of my kindred, and of my father's house."

> Gen 24:41 *Then shalt thou be clear from this my oath when thou comest to my kindred; and if they give not thee one, thou shalt be clear from my oath.*

Marriage is established with all parties agreeing. And this agreement is no simple add-on feature of marriage. Remember the time of your salvation. God was seeking you, and you were seeking God. God does not force or trick you into wanting Him.

He wants a proper relationship. The fact is Jesus wants an eternal relationship as does the Bride of Christ. Non-permanence is the core failure of the Baby Boomers' lack of marital arrangement. It is a big part of the growing deception. All the nineteen-sixty alternate forms of "marriage" arrangements have a deficiency dealing with permanence for a lifetime. The Boomers' approach was, "Give it a try and see how it works." With no lasting commitment, a lack of trust was introduced. Here today, gone tomorrow. The result is in that song: One is the loneliest number since the number two.

Isaac and Rebekah's freedom here is to make a final choice. To say yes or no forever. It is not, an "okay, let's try it" relationship. What Eliezer is doing is moving the marriage proposal away from the physical and emotional. It is the Spiritual side of dating or decision making that must drive the process. It changes the concept from dating for fun to... dating to prove all things.

> Gen 24:42 *And I came this day unto the well, and said, O Lord God of my master Abraham, if now thou do prosper my way which I go;*

The next step is to pray. And Eliezer did: *"O Lord ...if now thou do prosper my way which I go."* The first step was to find a mate (we call it dating) with spiritual guidance. If Eliezer had stopped here, the process might have stalled out at the start. When God sends an angel before us to prepare the way, we must also stay in *"the way."* If we are not paying attention, we may not see what God is doing. Remember the world's suggestions and answers must be removed from the dating mentality. No Canaanite ways are allowed as you prove all things. If you are going to date people who are not committed to God, don't expect them to suddenly change overnight and become a righteous or virtuous person just for you. The temptation to bait and switch is ever present when you use only the physical and emotional attractions of modern romance methods. You may be deceived.

Start looking for a spiritual connection and allow God time to prepare the way. A lifetime of marital bliss is worth the wait. You do not need a complicated test on the same level Eliezer used. There are many Biblical ways to prove "all things" presented in the Bible. These ways will help expose the lie. But you must be willing to see the truth.

> Gen 24:43 *Behold, I stand by the well of water; and it shall come to pass, that when the virgin cometh forth to draw water, and I say to her, Give me, I pray thee, a little water of thy pitcher to drink;*

Does this sound familiar? It should; it is from verse 24:14 Why is it repeated twice in the same chapter? God's word is always very much to the point. Why repeat? Perhaps it is to make sure we got the message. When you tell somebody something two times it is because you want to make sure they got it. And that is what you find in the Bible. But here I think there is something more. If we consider the audience, her family, they do not know what has happened. This story will also be told one more time to Isaac. When we arrive at the end of the story, it's not "Here is your bride." Isaac will also hear all the story and learn how Rebekah is the one God has prepared and why. The spiritual part once again takes the front driver's seat in the dating process.

Why does Scripture repeat the story?

- So we won't miss the point. Sometimes we are not paying attention.

- So her parents could see why it had to be Rebekah. They needed to know the full story.

- So Rebekah would know why she was the right girl. This is probably one of the main reasons.

- So we can see the story from her family's viewpoint. The fullness of what God is doing.

Eleven

Rebekah's Part in the Process of Dating

Gen 24:43-46 *Behold, I stand by the well of water; and it shall come to pass, that when the virgin cometh forth to draw water, and I say to her, Give me, I pray thee, a little water of thy pitcher to drink;*

And she say to me, Both drink thou, and I will also draw for thy camels: let the same be the woman whom the Lord hath appointed out for my master's son.

And before I had done speaking in mine heart, behold, Rebekah came forth with her pitcher on her shoulder; and she went down unto the well, and drew water: and I said unto her, Let me drink, I pray thee.

And she made haste, and let down her pitcher from her shoulder, and said, Drink, and I will give thy camels drink also: so I drank, and she made the camels drink also.

We are now entering the part of the story where Rebekah is going to have a chance to use the same rules of dating we should apply today. Of course, the big difference here is Isaac is miles away. If your mind goes to Internet dating services– watch out. The Internet is full of deception. People who post about themselves can say anything, whether true or not, and nobody will know. So how is this different than Rebekah not having met Isaac? In all depends on how you look at the story.

The actual events at the "well" were a group of simple tests to show God was involved. And it is easy to see God was at work. The nature of this young girl named Rebekah was also apparent. What made her "tick?" How she was wired was easy to see. Her freely watering ten camels speaks volumes compared to seeing her sit on a front porch in a fancy dress waiting for prince charming to sweep her off her feet.

Rebekah now for the first time is seeing they were watching what she had done. She now understood they were looking for a specific girl. If God was involved, what were they looking to see in her? The question on her mind most likely was, "Do I fit what they are searching to find, or are they looking for somebody else?"

Rebekah begins to understand they want a girl who has maintained her purity – a virgin. The narrator has told us in two ways so no misunderstanding can be had. What God wanted was a virtuous woman, a virgin, neither had any man known her. We need to keep in mind the bloodline of the Seed. Rebekah was qualified.

She now knows the request given to her was a test. My guess is she probably saw it as a "nothing test." Who would not give a thirsty person a drink? In Genesis 24:15, it seems after Eliezer's prayer, Rebekah stepped into the story. I doubt if she realized being the first girl to the well also screamed out the truth of who she was. I suspect that most teens, boy or girl, would be trying to put off the chore of watering camels. Not, Rebekah – she was first on the scene.

Here is some dating "test" material to see if you or the person you are considering spending time with can prove all things. The answers to these questions tell the condition of "self."

- How do you obey your parents, or your employer. How do you obey Jesus? If it is disrespect, disobedience, procrastination, or laziness, then you most likely fail the water-the-camel test.

- Do you have the tools to pass "the worthy" test? Rebekah did. Do you pray? Do you read the Bible because you want to? If you are weak spiritually, then you may be easily deceived. If you are not looking for spiritual signs, you will never see them. You "fine tune" your skills by reading the stories in the Bible. The Bible has many examples of "failure to prove all things." Learn to identify them.

- How do you love the brethren? – John 13:35 - *By this shall all men know that ye are my disciples if ye have love one to another.*

- Do you have a burden for the unsaved of this world? The world needs a drink of Living Water. What's in your pitcher?

This is not as hard as you may think. God is not looking for perfection, but He is looking to see our heart's desire. If we do not want Jesus active in our lives, the person we want to find may never see us.

In my story and experience in dating, it was when I realized I was looking at somebody that loved the Lord that changed my plans for marriage. I went from "someday" God might show me who I am to marry - to maybe I had better be paying attention. Is she the one? I can't tell you what I saw in her actions, but I knew I was looking at a person I would want to date because she was the kind of person I would want to be with the rest of my life. After fifty years I can say what I "saw" was "she would water ten camels if they needed watering," because she would.

Gen 24:43 *Behold, I stand by the well of water; and it shall come to pass, that when the virgin cometh forth to draw water, and I say to her, Give me, I pray thee, a little water of thy pitcher to drink;*

God's plan for marriage includes the entire family. They needed to know what Rebekah had done and what Eliezer had told her. I wonder if Rebekah's hard work came as a surprise to them or was it her normal behavior to serve those in need? My guess is her family knew her ways, and it didn't surprise them at all. But ten camels would be over the top for anybody. Her behavior was outstanding, even if it was what she would typically do.

What had Rebekah seen that moved her graciousness into such a difficult task? There is a "one-word" answer: "need."

As we read the story of Abraham, God has recorded the events of Abraham's life as they happened. What is missing is the hype we are so accustomed to in our media-controlled world. It is so understated in Genesis 24:1 and 24:35 that we could miss what it means. We do not pay much attention to how wealthy and powerful Abraham was in his country. Abraham was a righteous man, and as a result, he was given great respect to go with his wealth. He was a very influential man.

As pictured before, we should look at the ten camels arriving as ten, black, governmental SUVs. When they pulled up, Rebekah knew something big was happening. With just a limited number of words and actions, she knew God was doing something big. It got her attention. Rebekah was beginning to see that her natural response, or maybe we should say spiritual response, at the "well" was something that reflected her passion for doing things right. I wonder if when she got to camel number five, she began to think she had made a mistake? Nope, Rebekah was doing necessary and essential work, and she knew it.

As Rebekah was taking all this in, so was her family. They all needed to catch up to what was happening. Abraham was God's prophet on the earth at this time, and even a girl who carried water could discern this.

I wonder if the fact that Eliezer was considering her actions as something Isaac would want in a wife heightened her interest? She could not see Isaac, but she saw through Eliezer, who knew him well, and she was impressed. In my experience fifty years ago, my heart skipped a few beats as the Spirit of truth said,

"Take note of this." And I did.

I must insert a critical item here. Rebekah was not looking for her soul-mate. She was busy doing what she needed to do for her family. When you are letting God direct your search for a lifelong companion, my guess is the best way to do it is to be who you are, and "the one" will find you at the same time you see "the one." When "proving all things," notice the qualities of the person. Are they God's representative on earth? But, test all things. As a youth pastor, I would tell the teens, "Just because a person walked out of the Christian Bookstore on the Mall doesn't mean they are the right one. But then again, it is certainly not a bad thing. It might be a starting point of interest.

> Gen 24:44 *And she say to me, Both drink thou, and I will also draw for thy camels: let the same be the woman whom the Lord hath appointed out for my master's son.*

Rebekah was aware of what she had said and done. I wonder if she had ever seen anyone else go out of their way to help others on this level, especially for nasty camels. Sinful human nature is to serve self first and serve others if you can get something out of it. Could she see what she did identified her as the one God had chosen? If Rebekah did not already know, she soon became aware that her actions were something of which God approved. If you have spent any time in God's Word, discipleship, or around church people, then you already have some thoughts on the things of which God approves and disapproves.

If you are not born-again, this could all sound as confusing as chemistry class was for me. You can start with the Appendix in the back to learn what is meant by "born-again" or "The meaning of discipleship? You can find a church that teaches the Bible. I highly recommend one-on-one discipleship. If your church doesn't have an organized ministry for discipleship, look around and find a spirit-filled person. They are easy to spot and always happy to help. If your concern is marriage, find a couple that is centered on God and seek some of their secrets. Don't expect to find perfection, but if you listen closely, you will hear that somewhere God was involved in the dating-marriage relationship. Seek the stories about success to see how they did it.

> Gen 24:45 *And before I had done speaking in mine heart, behold, Rebekah came forth with her pitcher on her shoulder; and she went down unto the well, and drew water: and I said unto her, Let me drink, I pray thee.*

Can you hear the excitement in Eliezer's voice inside the narrative? If books had a soundtrack, you would notice the change in tempo. "Before I had done speaking in mine heart" is a fantastic statement. This sounds like the magic formula to me. But remember, it all started weeks prior with prayer, and it had been non-stop throughout all those long weeks of travel. It was a miraculous meeting. It certainly was not a microwave event. I suspect Abraham and his wife Sarah had prayed for years for the right soul-mate for Isaac.

A great marriage may not just start in heaven; it may have roots here on earth with someone down on their knees. I have seen this with my children. My wife was praying for their future spouses from the time they were born, and God answered her prayers. Her prayers have now moved to grandchildren. I can't wait to see how God will answer these prayers.

Look at the simple beginning of this story, everybody heard it. A simple request for help opened the door to generation after generation of believers in God. What if Rebekah had taken a lackadaisical approach and said, "I don't feel like it, help yourself, I have to get back home." Or what if she had headphones on or was texting while watering? If Rebekah has not been the person she was, there would be no Genesis Twenty-four story, no match made in heaven, and we would not have this biblical guide in Genesis to marriage. If Rebekah had not been at the right place at the right time, we would have nothing. If God's hand is in it,

He will place us in the right place at the right time. We do not have to worry about it.

This is a not so hidden hint. Lonely people get nothing when they invest all their time on video games, movies, social media, and the many other solo activities the World System has created to keep them away from meeting their soul-mate. Find out where God is doing something and join in with spiritual eyes wide open. It may surprise you how easy it can be.

Be prepared and stay equipped to meet unexpected needs. I'm talking about things like reading the Bible every day. Read it, study it, meditate on it, and love it. You will soon need what you find.

> Gen 24:46 *And she made haste, and let down her pitcher from her shoulder, and said, Drink, and I will give thy camels drink also: so I drank, and she gave the camels a drink also.*

Don't forget to go the extra mile. Serve when you see something is needed. But don't fake it. You can't fake integrity. The Baby Boomers saw the hypocrisy of the "Great Generation" because of their lack of concern for racism based on skin color. You can't hide your core beliefs. But God's Words can change people.

Those who have never voluntarily gone out of their way to help others in need should try it. There is no greater joy than knowing things were made better for another by solving an issue they could not do themselves.

Here are a couple of "big" test questions on dating readiness.

1. BIG TEST #1: Do you have a pattern of compromising the rules so "self " can have its way.

2. BIG TEST #2: Do you consider yourself to be a "missionary" to those around you? Do you see the consequences your life has had on others?

Nobody is perfect, but we should have a desire to be made perfect. If the answers to the two questions above indicate that you or your kids are not ready to date, then seek Scripture on the issues in which there is a struggle.

For example, if porn is an issue, put some verses together and see that porn is really adultery and you are hurting other people. The "clicks" you make are keeping a young woman held hostage by her evil brokers. Pornography is a major killer of marital relationships. Seek help.

Pray for personal understanding and growth in weak areas.

Everybody has weak areas in their life, and things that may not even seem directly related to marriage but nevertheless may be troublesome. If you are concerned, make some effort to address them. Weak areas are usually connected to a lack of trust in God and what He has said. Adam and Eve didn't believe what God said about dying if they ate the forbidden fruit. They were wrong, and God was right.

Find a believer who will disciple you. It costs nothing but a little time. Find a person who truly believes in God and they will, like Rebekah, give you some Living Water.

God's Spirit will give discernment to that which is right. Jesus sent an angel before Eliezer to prepare the way for the marriage of Isaac and Rebekah. And He can do the same for you.

Twelve

Who Are You?

Gen 24:47-48 And I asked her, and said, Whose daughter art thou? And she said, The daughter of Bethuel, Nahor's son, whom Milcah bare unto him: and I put the earring upon her face, and the bracelets upon her hands.

And I bowed down my head, and worshipped the Lord, and blessed the Lord God of my master Abraham, which had led me in the right way to take my master's brother's daughter unto his son.

If you find the Bible (and this story) seems to repeat things over and over, take it as one of the hints I am always pointing out. We need to do the same with dating. Take time, so all will know that God is involved in your dating - HINT, repeat your story about God to everyone.

One of the reasons God is left out of most dating stories is nobody could see how God was involved. Just because someone did not see it, doesn't mean He was not involved. If you are reading this story and know how God was involved in your dating and later marriage – tell the story over and over. People need to hear it.

Gen 24:47 And I asked her, and said, Whose daughter art thou? And she said the daughter of Bethuel, Nahor's son, whom Milcah bare unto him: and I put the earring upon her face and the bracelets upon her hands.

As we near the end of Eliezer's recap of the first meeting at the well, we see a restatement of the family connection with God. This God-centered process was the best way to find Isaac a bride as far removed from the Canaanite idolatry as possible. Abraham and Nahor's parents came out of Ur, a land where people served other gods. But Abraham believed God, and He had shared his belief with his family. As a result, this family is different. They knew there was only one God, not multiple false gods as was so prevalent in their culture. Abraham's search for Isaac's wife in his family tells me they believed, at least at one time, in the One True God. To avoid the pagan influence of false do-nothing-gods, the convenience of finding a local bride was rejected. Isaac's bride needed to come from the family line back in Mesopotamia.

Our culture today may lose the "spiritual" significance of this story for at least two reasons. Firstly because of marrying a cousin, a relationship which was acceptable to God in those days, and secondly, the lack of belief in the spiritual things of God. Spiritual things are considered mystical at best by most people. So, the fact that Abraham would go to such lengths to secure a wife for spiritual reasons is unbelievable by contemporary standards.

Once again, we are about to see the storyteller of Genesis Twenty-four move the topic back to spiritual considerations. We find that Rebekah's family will use it in considering the marriage proposal.

How does this apply to 21st Century dating practices? I would guess by now that you would be expecting some application. It is the same one from the start. We marry the people we date. So, who should we date? The best answer is a spiritually growing, born-again Christian who believes the Bible. This narrows the field. The control goes to God. If we are God-seekers, we must look for a person who is faithful to God and his purposes.

Here are some Scriptures to search.

- 2 Cor 6:14 – Be ye not unequally yoked.

- 1 Pet 2:9-10 – Be a peculiar people

- Rom 15:5 – Be patient.

- Phil 2:2 & 20 – Be like-minded.

- 2 Tim 1-9 – Be Holy.

- Rev 17:14 – Be Faithful before and after.

- Rom 12:1 – Be a Living Sacrifice.

Proverbs 25:19 is especially important. It says "*confidence in an unfaithful man in time of trouble is like a broken tooth, and a foot out of joint.*" Marriage, even the best ones, are full of tensions. Make sure the person you date is faithful to God, showing you what will happen when pressure is applied.

Here is another personal test: The person you should date is the person you should be.

Eliezer now mentions the gold jewelry. The KJV says earring upon her face, and I see earrings on her ears. But most translations say, "nose ring." I am sorry, but for me that doesn't work. I see no beauty in that. Nevertheless, I know from the Hebrew it was a nose ring. If we stop and think about it, fashion trends are often not attractive. We are taught what is in style and desirable by designers. We are swayed by the people who are selling their ideas. Apparently, nose rings were the deal. I can make a long list of fashions-trends I don't quite understand, especially from the nineteen-sixties. I offer bell-bottom pants as my example. They keep coming back and then rapidly go away. It is my personal opinion, but I am not a fan of the nose ring or other trends that come and go.

The gold jewelry created various reactions with those that saw it. Different, yet the same. For Rebekah who received it,

I believe she was duly impressed that something was about to happen that went beyond watering camels. As I have hinted, her brother and father may have had a different reaction. It is possible they just saw an opportunity to get rich quick.

Some people see wealth as personal power and the ability to buy more glitz. Others may see wealth as an opportunity to help those in need. I think for Rebekah, she just assumed that something big was about to happen. Go back and notice her words in verse 24:28. The only mention of the jewelry was when her brother saw it. Rebekah had much to tell beyond what they could see. My guess is the prayer and worship of God in verse 24:26 caught her attention – it would for me.

Gen 24:48 *And I bowed down my head, and worshipped the Lord, and blessed the Lord God of my master Abraham, which had led me in the right way to take my master's brother's daughter unto his son.*

Worship was not lost in the story by Eliezer. It was his focus, and now he made it the center of the conversation. Rebekah was remarkable for her performance. The jewelry was magnificent. But the significant point is what God's angel had done. All involved were blessed by what God had prepared. Eliezer knew he had been led the right way to find the correct wife for Abraham's son, Isaac.

We just saw a power play that will establish the rest of the story. If we take God out, it is still a beautiful story. But if we leave God in the story and focus on what God is doing, it becomes a magnificent narrative. It shows God working among His Creation. If we had music, this is the time for it to grow soft while the matter was under consideration of everyone there.

It is almost time for the question.

Will they approve or not? There is an application here for dating. All parents and spiritual leadership should accept the person we are dating. While this remains true for everybody, it is especially true for teens: the younger the teen, the more important the effort and time spent searching for the truth. A primary consideration is the spiritual value of this relationship.

I did very little dating as a young man. I still consider this a good thing. As a youth pastor for several years, the only result I saw dating produce was heartbreak and pain. The results of dating too young can scar a person for life. Young children and teens can be brutal in the way they treat each other. It is a process of power plays and self-esteem building at the expense of another. I have never seen any value in "one-on-one" dating for most teens. However, group gatherings with proper guidelines can build well-balanced adults.

I should mention here the spiritual condition of parents and others in leadership positions. Again, watch out for private agendas. Our world has bought "The Lie." Some of the worst enemies of proper spiritual dating are parents or friends pushing a child into awkward situations. Warped thinking from the pastor the media blitz of shallow relationships controls most of modern thinking. Being popular is nothing compared to being happy for 50 years of marriage.

For the more mature adult, a parent may well be out of the picture. So, build connections with people who are tracking with God. Seek their advice, take time before saying yes to a date. If restraint is shown in deciding who to date, then the process of making sure dating situations go the "right way" has already been established.

Here are some Scriptures to search.

• Eph 6:1- Obey- does not mean just small children.

- Col 3:20 – This is pleasing to the Lord.

- Gal 4:1-2 – A child is a child.

- Rom 13:1-2 – Everyone is subject to a higher power.

Remember, God has given man free-will and He respects our choices, even if they are wrong. He is not vengeful if we neglect His ways. But God will also personally suffer from the mistakes made by a terrible choice. Just like our earthly parents suffer from the wrong choices of their children, He desires the best for His Creation. God designed His kingdom of people in His image and likeness to function in the same way He does. If we ignore His ways of righteousness, expect difficulty.

Our story will start to move quickly now. The process that has brought us to this point has taken months to happen. The dating process is over in Rebekah's story. The events at the well and with the family later proved all things. It is time for a decision. It has been a family concern from the beginning. Now it is time for the family to agree. Rebekah has seen she is not being forced. Her decision will be a free choice. It is time to see how Nahor's family, including Rebekah, will respond to what God is doing.

Modern dating has flipped the reasoning process for marriage. The Baby Boomer's rebellion shifted the focus to very temporary things, physical and emotional things which are always changing. But a spiritual connection remains fixed and constant. It is what binds a marriage and allows a couple to overcome the never-ending drama of life.

Thirteen

Decision Time

*Gen 24:49-54 And now if ye will deal kindly and truly with my
master, tell me: and if not, tell me; that I may turn to the right hand,
or to the left.*

*Then Laban and Bethuel answered and said, The thing
proceedeth from the Lord: we cannot speak unto thee bad or good.*

*Behold, Rebekah is before thee, take her, and go, and let her be thy
master's son's wife, as the Lord hath spoken.*

*And it came to pass, that, when Abraham's servant heard their
words, he worshipped the Lord, bowing himself to the earth.*

*And the servant brought forth jewels of silver, and jewels of
gold, and raiment, and gave them to Rebekah: he gave also to her
brother and to her mother precious things.*

*And they did eat and drink, he and the men that were with him,
and tarried all night; and they rose up in the morning, and he said,
Send me away unto my master.*

Eliezer has presented Isaac's need for a wife, the significance
of the Covenant family, and God's involvement. All are
established. He has shown how Rebekah, without pre-knowledge,
is God's choice. The food is getting cold on the table, but a
decision must be reached. It is a similar process to our salvation.

All things must stop, and you must decide.

*Gen 24:49 And now if ye will deal kindly and truly with my
master, tell me: and if not, tell me; that I may turn to the right hand,
or to the left.*

I find Eliezer's last appeal fascinating: *"And now if ye will deal kindly and truly with my master."* For the first time, we see that emotion enters the story. Isaac has needs that are both emotional and physical. It is not good that man is alone. What would happen to God's plan if they all said no? Would the story end here for the kingdom God has planned? What a silly and unneeded question. God knew Rebekah's heart when he chose her.

The long-distance romance of Rebekah and Isaac may seem strange to us, but it shouldn't. For those who are born-again, the same kind of situation is seen with Jesus Christ. When we said yes to His offer of eternal Salvation, we did so with the same type of information Rebekah had. We have not seen Jesus face to face, but we know He is the one in which we want to spend all eternity.

When God created mankind, he had a plan called marriage. There are, however, some who have the spiritual gift to remain single, but for most God has planned a lifetime of marriage with oneness and purpose. Where God is intentionally part of the process, you have spiritual dating, and there will come a time when all things are apparent to everyone. It is here that emotion should enter the picture – not before. Test all things before dating. If God is not involved in the process, then the process is not of God. Don't expect dating and marriage to work well without God's involvement.

If you have experienced pain and suffering from emotional and physically based dating, then detox your system and start over. God can point you in the right direction. Get into the Bible. Re-read this story over and over until you see the spiritual side. Study out some of the things in the Appendix. Turn your loneliness over to God.

Warning: do not expect to find a perfect sequence of events as Eliezer found. "The Lie" has touched us all. Remember, perfection is not the goal. If God demanded perfection, nobody would qualify. What we are trying to find is somebody who is seeking God and God's ways. Isaac had a relationship with God, and Rebekah's heart was in tandem with God. But family and friends will often get in the way. They also have plans for your life. We will get a hint of this in the narrative that follows.

In my own story, it was the spiritual realization that I was looking for a young lady that had her heart lined up with God. I knew my desires to be involved in the Lord's work would not sit well with a lot of young women in my culture. As we slowly started dating, it was the revelation of a similar spiritual direction that moved us forward in our romance. Both of our families were supportive. In a six-month period, two people who were not seeking to get married discovered their soul-mates.

Tell me or tell me not – "I need an answer before I move on" was the play on the table.

Eliezer was not going to give up if he hit a roadblock that stopped this story. Maybe Rebekah was an accident and not the right girl. What he needed was approval from the family based on what God was doing.

What would they say about this enormous request to give up a daughter, a sister, to an almost unknown person who lived far, far away? The family was more than aware that they had not seen Isaac, and they recognized they would probably never see Rebekah again if they said yes. If there had been background orchestration, it would now stop. In silence, we wait for the answer.

Gen 24:50 *Then Laban and Bethuel answered and said, The thing proceedeth from the Lord: we cannot speak unto thee bad or good.*

The answer contains the essential words; the thing proceedeth from the Lord. We see this as good news, but it came with a new and somewhat startling revelation. Rebekah's father, Bethuel, has been suspiciously missing from the narrative. It may not seem strange to you, but traditionally, the father is the major player in the marriage of a daughter. And he has just now shown up?

Rebekah's father barely made the story, and this is his only point of entry into the process. To me, it stands out as strange. Where had he been, and why is he only here for these few words. Why such a small a part? I tried to research it and found a few suggestions but none with much biblical support. But I did discover a reason. I am going to move this discussion to later because it interrupts our storyline at this point.

There is a little, hidden problem embedded here. Both families approved of the marriage. Marriage, in a perfect world, would have the agreement of the entire family. And that is what we see in this verse. Dad appears briefly, and his reply follows his son's answer. Bottom line, they both agree – I think. They were brilliantly correct in saying, "this came from the Lord." They both recognize it as so. But then we have a fuzzy byline added. They could not see "good" or "bad" with what has transpired.

Most Bible translations leave this as "cannot speak either good or bad" as found in the KJV. In some modern translations it has been translated as:

- We can say nothing to you one way or another. NIV

- We have no choice in the matter. CSB

- There is nothing we can say. NLT

Most people seem to think that this means it was so obvious that there was no reason to object. I would agree if the two said they could not see any "bad" about what had happened. But they also said they could not see "good." Flag down on the play for me. When God is behind something, what would not be good?

Everything that had happened was a "good thing." God never does evil. Nevertheless, the son and father did not rule out bad things as a possibility. If you can't see the good or bad, what do you see? When God is involved, the logical conclusion is that it is an eternally good thing. It appears they were not sure or indifferent.

Here is another hidden dating guideline you should note in the dating process. A date is to be a good thing, not neutral, and certainly not a bad thing. Dating is the method of testing to see what is true — deception rules in a fallen world. If we don't test and prove all things, don't be surprised if we don't get what we were hoping to find. The old saying "love is blind" doesn't apply to the dating process. Spiritual eyes must be wide open. It is our life of joy at stake. One may be lonely, but two can be a nightmare if deception is used to form the union.

There might be a hint of private desire in the answer of Laban and Bethuel. If we look ahead at Laban's character in what happens years later with Jacob, we see he is not always what he pretends to be. Laban was a very good "scammer." Were his eyes focused on all the money? Can we read the story as if Laban had hoped to get a reward for what he did?

I do not believe that Rebekah's head was "turned" by the jewels. The son and father's comment about good or bad lines up with a person who might have a private and preferred plan but couldn't go against all the evidence that God was at work. God at work has this effect on things. What He does is so brilliant that evil must duck and cover and wait for another day.

When it comes to dating, there is often a private agenda. Our goal is to be a person focused on doing right, like Rebekah, and not on what we can get out of others. Parents and close friends can get in the way. But if we point out what God is doing, others will have to park their opinions and agree with what God is doing.

If we leave God out of the story, others have an open playing field to run schemes. For example, watch some of the "G" rated romance movies. There is always somebody who has other plans for the couple. Don't go to the movies for marital advice they make movies to make money. God's guidance is also for only one reason, to have a kingdom of people who desire to live abundantly and full of joy. Hollywood is only taking; God is only giving.

So, how will we know when the right person stands before us? How will God speak to us? Rebekah's astonishing story is filled with big dollars and a real prince and princess as the players. The way we recognize who is "right" is the same – prove all things.

God will show us in such a way that we will have no doubt. Don't be deceived, prove all things. When God is at work, all people will know. If a flag comes down on the play, stop and move slowly. We can hear the still small voice of God if we control our "out of control" physical and emotional desires. The more Bible we know, the better our chances of knowing God's direction in our life. But as I stated in my own story, I did not understand a lot of the Bible, but I made sure attention was given to what I did know - like young Daniel.

God talks to us through His written Word. At work or school, we will hear somebody ask, "What does the boss or teacher say about this." Chances are we already know. Likewise, if we know what the Bible says, we know what God wants, and what He would have us do. Filtering thoughts and actions through God's Written Word will make life easier and joy-filled.

God's ways do not limit our "fun." They just enable us to have "fun" that is more meaningful and lasts a long time. An Eternal God finds little joy in brief and temporary "fun." His way just happens to be the only way life works correctly. He designed it all; He alone knows the best way to experience what He created.

It all depends on what we want to put in our head. Hollywood's thinking will probably end in loneliness. God's ways will lead to family.

Gen 24:51 *Behold, Rebekah is before thee, take her, and go, and let her be thy master's son's wife, as the Lord hath spoken.*

Here is their answer to the marriage proposal – "take her." It sounds harsh, don't you think?

To lose a daughter, a sister to marriage is not an easy thing, but the definition of marriage says, "leave." Marriage is the beginning of a new family. Rebekah was not only loved as a family member, but she was also an important part of their everyday life. I see why they might have said: "take her." I felt this as my two sons married, but I also gained two daughters-in-law. And then came the beautiful gift, grandchildren.

One of the things that people often lose out on by not raising a God-centered family is a close relationship with their grandchildren. To hold them and watch them grow up after your having gained wisdom from many years of life, you will see a deeper joy contained only in the family. I can see my wife, my sons, and myself in my grandchildren. I can see the image and likeness in which they were born into my family. I understand why God created us in His image and likeness. It is a good thing a marriage starts a new family.

In Rebekah's story, someone else will have to carry the water from the well. It is not about the jewelry and nor is it about losing control. But these may be key points for Rebekah's brother and father. Nevertheless, there is only one thing that should be considered. God has a more significant mission in mind for Rebekah and Isaac.

Jesus is one day going to take his Bride known as the Church away from their families on earth. It is in 1 Thessalonians 4:17 where we read that we will be "caught up" together in the clouds. "Caught up" sounds a lot like "take her." And it should. As I said, marriage is a picture of what God is doing on earth. If you look at Rebekah's story in the focus of Jesus and His Bride, you may see why I say this.

There will always be physical and emotional desires in the

dating process. But if we approach dating in a biblical fashion and seek the Spirit of Truth as we go, we have a greater chance of finding and living an entire life with a soul-mate.

Moving back to the story, we should not be the least bit surprised at what happens next.

> Gen 24:52 *And it came to pass, that, when Abraham's servant heard their words, he worshipped the Lord, bowing himself to the earth.*

God was praised and worshiped for His involvement. Is this what we expected? Be real here, if we were in that room what would be the predictable reaction? Ladies might say congratulations were in store for Rebekah. And that would be proper on such an exciting day. I'm still asking, what happened to dinner, are we going to skip eating? While both are typical reactions to the newly agreed upon marriage before meal time, one person reacted correctly. Eliezer. He turned the story to the Creator and director of the story. It says he "bowed to the ground." Ouch, in front of people? I know we're all thinking that's not going to happen today. Worship can be private, but if we don't pass "value" to God for who He is or what He has done, we need to consider why not. If we don't trust Him, I can see why we might want to keep it quiet. If we have fashioned our lives to conform to the world, we might want to hide our worship.

Bowing down is not part of most cultures today. Bowing is an act of submission, which is another thing we do not do well. It's part of the Boomer Rebellion. Submission to another is not what we are taught to do. If you hide your worship to God, then you are submitting to the pressures of Satan's World System. When you go into debt to impress somebody else about how well you are doing, you are worshiping the deception that glitzy stuff makes you who you are.

God made you who you are. What are you doing with what he created?

What should our worship be? We can't fake it. When we begin to trust God, we will start to see what He is doing all around us. When we experience God, our faith grows, and we will find ourselves worshiping God in ways we never saw possible. Worship is a natural expression of thanks for what God has done. If we must hide our worship, then it might be because we have not experienced what God is doing.

I did not make up this old story in Genesis; it is several thousand years old. I also did not make up the story about the marriage I have been blessed to have. From the time I was saved, I desired to be where God is doing something. And I have seen many incredible things. You can't see what God is doing if you are not looking or living to see it.

God is the Creator and director of this story. Is God the Creator and director of your story? Or are you the one in control? If you do not see the Holy Spirit as the guide for your life, then where are you getting your wisdom? If you evaluate "how" you make decisions, you can see why you get the results you get.

Don't lie to yourself about being happy if you are not. If you struggle to get through each day, find out why. A good guess is most people are using the stuff arranged by the world to help them escape life as it happens. Comfort food and drugs are common ways to survive, but not helpful in living a full and happy life. Living God's way does not require these crutches.

Satan desires to refocus our eyes, as he did with Eve. Satan directed Eve's eyes to something she did not need to be considering. When she looked at the forbidden fruit, she saw that it looked good for food. His next step was to misrepresent the truth. He lied and told her she would not die. She would be as a god. He deceived her into wanting something she should not have. She didn't need more food, nor did she need to be as a god. Satan was tempting her with more than she was given. And she bought "The Lie." And I suspect happiness eluded her most of her life.

You can see the same trick in every television show, movie,

advertisement, and most music. You may not need a new wardrobe, a shiny new car, or a bigger fancier house, but "lust of the eyes" will tell you that you will look good in that.

No matter how you view your soul-mate, Hollywood has redefined the terms handsome and beautiful to a non-practical standard. If you see Hollywood's best stars outside of their glamorous wardrobes and makeup, they are just ordinary people. And I might point out, many of them use alcohol or some other kind of drug to keep up their act.

So, who is creating your story?

God is never too busy to help you write your life or romance story. He has already set everything in place. Are you paying attention to what God is doing in your life?

In John 10:10, Jesus said, "I have come that they may have life, and have it more abundantly. If you read the entire verse, you notice a warning about the thief. The thief is Satan and his World System. So, who is writing your story? To whom do you bow down? Where is your worship focused? It is your free choice.

Gen 24:53 *And the servant brought forth jewels of silver, and jewels of gold, and raiment, and gave them to Rebekah: he gave also to her brother and to her mother precious things.*

There is one more thing to be done before Rebekah's family eats. (Sounds like all the food will be cold.) Now that the agreement has been presented, she is about to see what happens when God blesses. He does so extravagantly beyond what anyone would expect. Rebekah was seeing that being part of the chosen family was abundantly good. More gold, more jewelry, and even her clothes were going to be different. I don't know if all this was necessary for her sake, but her family needed to know.

There is also an encrypted message to the Bride of Christ here. As we make that final move to heaven, these kinds of precious things will be everywhere. Even the streets will be gold. Gold and silver have a permanent nature to them. We will need permanent streets in heaven. Items made of paper, wood, and concrete are only temporary. It needs to be gold for an eternity in heaven. Rebekah got a little taste of what the Bride of Christ will see. We also get a new wardrobe, and it will be pure white.

Two things are getting ready to happen: bride-price and dowry. Here is what Wikipedia has to say.

The term "bride-price" is known as the bride token. It is money, property, or another form of wealth paid by a groom or his family to the parents of the woman he has just married or is just about to marry. Bride-price is similar to a dowry, which is paid to the groom or used by the bride to help establish the new household and dower, which is property settled on the bride herself by the groom at the time of marriage.

It continues and says, "Some cultures may practice both dowry and bride-price simultaneously. It seems to be a very old practice, perhaps common before existing records. I do not find a biblical mandate for paying for the bride, but it is in the Old Testament. There is a connection here with the concept of inheritance and God's definition of marriage. Since the Bride was leaving her family, none of her parent's estates would be coming her way; this is where we get the term dowry. At the same time, the family would be losing her substantial contribution and extra hands in the daily workload of the family. Rebekah's carrying of water would be a significant loss in their daily life.

So, the precious gifts from Abraham were very appropriate to his brother's family. Gifts to Rebekah's brother and mother, are perhaps connected to the custom of a "bride-price." What we see is an ancient custom which still has a trace in our culture today.

What I see is Abraham's generosity towards his brother's family for providing the perfect bride for the continuation of the Covenant family.

Rebekah's Father

Did you notice the omission of Rebekah's dad from the start of this story? Historically the father is a principal character in the marriage process. Is this a substantial and visible oversight? He finally appeared and made a statement with his son and agreed to the marriage. But look at what happened with the gifts. There were no gifts to him listed. Did he leave?

He is missing in several places. Rebekah went to her mother's house, not her father's house. We would expect her relationship to be closer to her mother, but as the story moves on, it moves to the brother, not the father. Since the father was alive, you would expect he would be deciding on the house guests. But perhaps he was sickly or too old and had left the management of the family affairs to his son. Strangely, the son's name is listed first. And now the father is not given a gift. I have looked through numerous commentaries and found no clear or satisfactory answer. What happened to the father in this story? He should be a significant player in the normal process of the marriage of a daughter. But not in this story.

He receives respect for his position as the father, but the omission of a more significant role as we would expect speaks volumes about the Editor in charge of Genesis chapter twenty-four. Marriage, in a perfect world, would have the agreement of the entire family. And that is what we see in this verse. Dad appears briefly and agrees.

Only one thing we know for sure this seems abnormal and hints of a dysfunctional family. God didn't tell us why, the father received no gifts, and other than his agreement about Rebekah's marriage, he is a non-player.

By not telling us why he is scarcely in the story, God has left it up to us to fill in the "why." This allows us to apply this in many kinds of situations in the marriage process. I think the point is his minimal mention. Bethuel, as the father, gives his input, but perhaps, in some way, he was dysfunctional or out of the picture. There may be cultural reasons for this, but it seems to say that the father was not a major participant in Rebekah's family life. At least not in this situation. However, her physical father was still given his rightful place to say what happens to his daughter.

There are several connections to the Church encoded here. Rebekah's story pictures many things about the marriage of the Bride of Christ. Accepting God's offer of salvation is the same as a marriage proposal. We left our old family and moved into the family of God. It is in this family in which we find great blessings. Satan is the acting ruler of the fallen family on earth, and he indeed is dysfunctional as the leader. And, Satan has no choice but to agree with God. I suspect he can't say if salvation is good or bad; it's too much for his evil mind to comprehend. But I am sure he doesn't like it.

And of course, there was the "bride-price" paid. Father God gave His only Son to secure the Bride of Christ. But like Bethuel, Satan is left out of the story and receives no gifts. Satan might as well agree because he knows Jesus is "taking" His Bride known as the Church.

God has stepped into the life of the family of Nahor, Abraham's brother, and things will never be the same.

> Gen 24:54 *And they did eat and drink, he and the men that were with him, and tarried all night; and they rose up in the morning, and he said, Send me away unto my master.*

Finally, they get to the meal. You probably think with all my talk about food and dinner being late, that food is a big part of life. If the truth be told, food is a big part of the story of all men. But a meal is nowhere near the importance of marriage.

Things are now ready. Rebekah's family can be sure that she is in good hands. Isaac will be a good husband and take care of his wife. There are many things required from the husband. If we try, we can construct a list of the Biblical Responsibilities of a Husband. This is a good place to insert one of them.

Responsibility number 5. To Provide for your wife.

1 Tim 5:8 - *But if any provide not for his own, and especially for those of his own house, he hath denied the faith, and is worse than an infidel.*

- To provide means more than just the basics: food, shelter, and clothing – it means all needs.

- It would include a feeling of security. Secure from physical danger, of needing basics, and knowledge you will always be there.

- This means providing, if possible, life insurance, disability insurance or a plan to care for her if you cannot do so in the future. See John 19:26-27.

- Make sure the tools needed to do the job correctly and efficiently are provided. Things like a washer, dryer, refrigerator, furniture, and all the rest of the stuff required to run a household. Here is a hint: This would come before the big 4-wheel drive or fancy bass boat.

- It means showing openly and privately your love for her.

- The man must fill the position of father to the children.

And don't forget this must include providing spiritually by keeping all the family in church.

These are the responsibilities that Isaac was going to take on with the new family he was going to form. If you read on in the story in Genesis, you will see that Isaac did provide for his family. He dug wells. He had great wealth and livestock, and his family needed water in a land not known for rain. Water is not on the list above, but it would be in the essential category. As a picture of Christ, Isaac was providing the water needed for his family. I see it as Living Water, don't you?

What a husband is to provide is one of the critical responsibilities that I had to consider some fifty years ago. And these are thoughts needed during the dating process. Both the man and the woman should understand that providing for each other is not optional. If there is no consideration of the needs of the other while dating, then you should not expect anything different later. The wife also has a list of responsibilities. Both "his" and "her" list of responsibilities will be at the end of this story.

Families of our present culture self-destruct because the man will not step up to the plate and provide for his family. I understand that sometimes, job roles today can be reversed. The issue is not who does what, but that each does his part to provide what is necessary. Family is about everybody contributing, not just taking what they want. It is to be a family of oneness.

After a good night's sleep, Eliezer is ready to finish the trip. We are almost out of the narrative, but there are still things to be accomplished. So, first thing in the morning, he asked his host permission to go back to Isaac. As always, an excellent servant uses only proper cultural etiquette. He was asking permission to start Rebekah on her journey. And now we will begin to see some "private agenda" sneak in and try to change God's plan. There will always be people trying to take advantage of what God is doing to benefit themselves.

Fourteen

Engagement

Gen 24:55 *And her brother and her mother said, Let the damsel abide with us a few days, at the least ten; after that she shall go.*

We might say the romance story of Isaac and Rebekah is now entering the "engagement period," although this is unusual because of the distance. The real engagement phase took place after she went and met Isaac. We see this in verse sixty-four. The engagement period of marriage starts after the proposal is accepted. So let's insert some biblical principles for the engagement part of marriage. We will come back to the story and see what you might be expecting - an interruption by the family. Yesterday they had agreed, but now they want to control the proceedings.

Some say that the engagement period is still a time of testing, but the Bible doesn't show this - engagement is final. All things should have been tested, proven, and finalized before the agreement to marry. Historically, in most parts of the world, what we have seen is arranged marriages — the decision of who married who was made by the parents. The ones getting married had little input in many cases. This process works great if God is part of the parental selection process. This is what we have seen in Rebekah's story. However, when God is taken out of the process of arranged marriages, it can become "business deals," and power plays based on "private agendas." For example, a house painter might arrange a wedding with a family that sells paint. There is not much romance in that kind of an arrangement.

Rebekah had opportunities to express her desires. She did run home and tell the news to her mother and brother. This was not an everyday occurrence. Someone had shown an interest in her. As the story of God unfolded, she was conscious of God at work, and this would be a marriage planned by God. I believe she understood that God was in all the praying, the worship, and gifts. She realized this was God-ordained and she was willing. Even in an arranged marriage, Rebekah had made her choice, and from that point, no other man on earth could turn her eyes. In the Hebrew custom, once the agreement was made, the couple was legally married. The engagement period was part of the final legal marriage.

We see this in the story of Mary and Joseph. The marriage agreement had been made, but Joseph and Mary had not come together. When he found that she was with child, Joseph sought to put her away privately - in other words, divorce. God once again stepped into the story and explained that this child had been conceived by the Holy Spirit – it was a miraculous conception. Joseph, a righteous man, understood and took the role of caring for the child. My point here is that engagement as seen by God was binding; it was the same as married. Espoused, betrothed or engaged was not a "testing time" to see if it worked. This is opposite and rather profound thinking compared to our current view of engagement today. Nevertheless, this is God's plan for a covenant marriage, and it works.

There are three parts to the marriage process: dating, engagement, and physical joining. Dating is the spiritual connection in marriage, engagement is the emotional connection, and the physical connection is on hold until after the ceremony. This process, presented in Rebekah and Isaac's story, is needed to produce a life-long marriage.

In our culture we sometimes see an engagement called off, implying that dating had not proved all things. It means that all things were not tested. Slow down, get it right. "Dating" God's way has a much better chance of ending successfully. Once the spiritual connection is made, the emotional bonding can begin. Bonding two souls together before an official agreement to stay together for life produces a ton of emotional pain if the relationship breaks up. Dating is not a bonding time; dating is the testing time. A lifelong commitment is started when two souls become spiritually glued together. God's plan for marriage has three parts for a reason. When you step outside His plan, emotional baggage lives on forever. When you think you have found your soul-mate but don't prove all things by jumping into a bonding process, guilt may haunt you later if things go bad.

The question is what went wrong when an engagement gets called off? The answer is obvious. All things were not proven. The reason was apparent before it was called off; those involved just did not understand or acknowledge it. Marriage should be a commitment for life. Those who can't commit, be it wandering eyes or a never satisfied desire, will reveal these tendencies in subtle ways during the dating process. Pay attention.

If you have kept the relationship non-physical, any bad tendencies should show up quickly. If you violate God's rules with a physical connection before marriage starts, expect to be fooled. A temporary physical bonding overpowers everything with a false sense of commitment. If you did not prove all things at the dating stage, then you will test all things after emotional bonding during the engagement and marriage. At this point, it is too late to just walk away without the additional damage of a failed marriage.

Rebekah had a proper proposal, but there was a considerable distance between her and her new husband. It's not in the biblical text, but I would not be surprised if Rebekah didn't ask Eliezer questions about Isaac as they were covering those many miles by camel. Because of cultural practices, it may not have happened. But can you imagine the "campfire" stories if they did talk? He could have told her many things about Isaac and

147

his family during those numerous days of travel. Hearing these stories would be the start of the emotional bonding process.

It is the same story of the Church. When we accepted the gift of salvation, we became His. The Father paid the price by giving His Son, and we accepted the proposal. Jesus is in Heaven preparing a place for his Bride. The Church has the Scriptures and the indwelling and unseen Spirit. As we hear the Bible stories, we too are preparing for the Marriage Supper of the Lamb.

We see a request for a delay in Rebekah's departure. Remember, everything that has happened did so in a very short time. By the way, rapid movement is not often the best approach for marriage. Moving quickly generally, leaves things untested and not proved. The dating and spiritual connection should proceed slowly over several months for most people.

We can emotionally see why a few days of preparation for the trip might be justified. A family may need time to adjust to what was taking place. Her family had very little reason to think they would ever see her again. As a family, they seemed to acknowledge what God was doing. But we also have seen a small hiccup in how the brother and father responded. As readers, we have no way of knowing what they were thinking, but we do learn about some undesirable traits of Laban years later. And we do know that Rebekah's father, who should have been a "mover-shaker" in this story, had only a cameo appearance. And he shared his only line with his son. For some unknown reason, God wrote him out of the story.

I agree with God. Rebekah needed to leave now with Eliezer before any con or scam could be hatched. We do not know that anything would have happened, but the way God tells Rebekah's story, there is much suspicion, at least on my part about the motives of Bethuel and Laban. I think we all understand the mother's desires for wanting a few extra days with her daughter.

Let's overview the entire process that should take place in forming a marriage.

Fifteen

Stages of Marriage and the Bigger Picture

Gen 24:56 *And he said unto them, Hinder me not, seeing the Lord hath prospered my way; send me away that I may go to my master.*

Marriage is God's plan to populate the earth. His goal is family. Both these institutions pre-picture the Kingdom coming and the family of God. After the fall in the Garden, there was no longer a spiritual connection to God. But God was prepared, so the need for a genuine marital relationship between a man and woman was hard-wired into our DNA. Even if a man can't spiritually understand his need for marriage, it is how we were designed. It is not good that man should be alone. In our culture dating is the normal first step in the relationship between a man and a woman who eventually marry. It is the same process between a person and Christ. Marriage is a picture of our salvation.

- A person is from a different family.

- A person realizes there is more to life then they have.

- A person seeks a change of direction in life.

- A proposal or offer of marriage (salvation) is given.

Engagement means the proposal is accepted. For Rebekah it was marriage. Her marriage was her salvation from loneliness.

Engagement

- The two begin to bond together emotionally into the same mind. (We are to have the mind of Christ.)

- Plans form for that day and the celebrations of the wedding. A change from the old life to the new begins to happen. (We die to the old life.)

- The focus and desire becomes the day of the wedding.

- A relationship is established, but physically there is a distance.

- The marriage day arrives, and a great celebration happens.

- The result is the dwelling together of those so long engaged.

It's a GREAT MYSTERY, but when accomplished, God's way of dating, engagement, and marriage produce an excellent picture for us. In contrast to all the correct relationship methods above, think about how God describes improper relationships in the Bible. He calls it harlotry and prostitution. Today's world system tries to soften these two words by describing them as "living together," or "hooked-up." But God's definitions remain the same, and His plan works as can be seen by the long-term effects of loneliness with the alternate approaches.

Delay Denied

We see that Rebekah's brother and her mother wanted her to stay a few more days, at least ten. After that, she could go. Personally, I see it as a very reasonable request, but there are concerns about Laban, as pointed out. And Eliezer was quite the spiritually driven man. Without even a discussion, Eliezer changes the story back to what God was doing. He moved away from emotions and possible stalls, to what God had already done. Pay attention; this is one of those big encoded hints on how to run your life. You can be emotionally driven, or you can be spiritually motivated. Emotions often lie to us. But the Spirit is truth. I am not the first to say that the Spirit is truth. It's all over the New Testament. For example, 1 John 5:6 and John 16:13 are two powerful ones.

> Gen 24:56 *And he said unto them, Hinder me not, seeing the Lord hath prospered my way; send me away that I may go to my master.*

Now that the dating phase is over and the agreement to marry is in place, the engagement period starts, and we see those who are trying to entangle Rebekah emotionally. This could be trouble.

A mother who genuinely loves her daughter can get in the way of what God is doing. Even Rebekah, years later, steps in to help God with the transfer of the blessing to her second son, Jacob. Some read this as Rebekah keeping her husband, Isaac, from making a mistake. I see it as Rebekah stopping a miracle of God. God had told Rebekah who the blessing was to go to, and God would have made it happen His way, but she interfered with what God was doing to hurry the process along and make sure herself. We will never know what God would have done. Emotions can get in the way of the truth.

Eliezer never gave the attempted ten-day dodge by Laban and his mother a chance to work as a delay. There is not one word in the story about why, but I think Eliezer, prompted by the Spirit of God, had read the body language of Rebekah's family and knew the motive behind their words. His request is well spoken; *"hinder me not."*

So, what should happen during the Engagement period,

knowing that it is not a place to test and prove all things? Engagement is not a trial marriage. It is a marriage without the physical.

Our culture suggests that engagement is just an opportunity to try out marriage, with a loophole to get out of what was agreed. In other words, there is no commitment at all. Marriage must be a lifelong commitment to produce family and avoid the garbage of divorce. We have seen that all critical decisions are made during the "spiritual" dating process, and engagement, like marriage, is permanent.

Sixteen

How Three Things Make One

Gen 24:57-62 *And they said, We will call the damsel, and inquire at her mouth.*

And they called Rebekah, and said unto her, Wilt thou go with this man?

And she said, I will go.

And they sent away Rebekah their sister, and her nurse, and Abraham's servant, and his men.

And they blessed Rebekah, and said unto her, Thou art our sister, be thou the mother of thousands of millions, and let thy seed possess the gate of those which hate them.

And Rebekah arose, and her damsels, and they rode upon the camels, and followed the man: and the servant took Rebekah, and went his way.

And Isaac came from the way of the well Lahai-roi; for he dwelt in the south country.

The Body, Soul, and Spirit of two people are to become one in a process called marriage. The better your understanding of what God is doing, the better your chances of getting it right. I did not know this process as a young man, but it is what happened over a year and a half of time and produced a marriage that has stayed strong.

First, we have the spirit part of dating. We start by building a spiritual base involving two souls and God. It is the seeking out and identifying process with God's help. It is to be done with Godly "eyes," using the Bible to see spiritually, not with human emotions. Dating is to build a spiritual base for a relationship. God must be involved. Like our salvation, it is a drawing out of words and actions. It is time for each to decide what they want. It is time to prove all things.

Scriptures to search:

- John 3:3-7 – Not physical.

- John 6:44, 45, 65 –Drawn spiritually.

- Matt 16:17 –Spirit reveals the truth, identifying who the soul-mate is to be.

Second, we have the soul part called engagement: Bonding together of two souls. It is a result of a question: Will you do this thing? It is like our Salvation experience. While it may vary with culture, a "yes" establishes the day of the marriage. Then you begin to grow emotionally together; to learn more about the other; to become like-minded. The concept of oneness is very different than being single. Issues that may surface are ironed out before the ceremony. The result is the beginning of bonding together, becoming soul mates – but still no physical relationship.

Scriptures to search:

- Gen 24:58 - She said yes.

- Acts 8:37 – Do you believe? – Will you go with Him?

- Rom 10:9-13 – Will you marry me? A "Yes" results in a confession with your mouth.

There is a longing to dwell together, to be together physically—a desire for the marriage day to come.

Third, is the physical marriage - being together as one. It is the final step in marriage, being together forever. We see this in Rev

19:9 And he saith unto me, Write, Blessed are they which are called unto the marriage supper of the Lamb. And he saith unto me, These are the true sayings of God. God has a special gift to those who marry. Have you noticed the "sexual" talk we hear so much today is not present in this Biblical discussion of marriage? That's because sexuality is a gift to two people, a private gift. We have no business even discussing it.

Satan has moved this physical part of marriage to the dating stage. By doing so, he destroys the picture God has given us. For the Church, the physical part comes at the end. The rapture of the Church is when the Saints receive their glorified bodies. How appropriate that it comes in this physical stage.

Eliezer stated the spiritual position very well. The music, if we had it, would now become tense. A "stall" could lengthen Rebekah's story by days, or even longer. But God had been at work. These events were not accidents, and they all knew it. However, just because God is in the story calling the shots doesn't mean that free choice cannot interrupt what God is doing. It happened page after page in the Bible, but not this time. Both Rebekah's mother and brother were ready to play their trump card. It was a sure thing, Rebekah could go, but they believed she would choose to stay a few days. What they failed to consider in their plan was what God had been doing in the life of Rebekah. She had made a spiritual choice. She was ready, and there was no turning back. I think it is a brilliant picture of Salvation. When we say yes to God's offer, there is nothing left in the world that would entice us to turn back or wait a few days.

Gen 24:57 *And they said, We would call the damsel, and inquire at her mouth.*

Rebekah Unaware

Rebekah was not aware, it seems, of this detour in yesterday's plan, suggested by her brother and mother. So as she entered the room, she had no concept what had transpired. Was the delay just Mom wanting more time or was this a scheme in the making?

This request, back in Genesis 24:55 to wait ten days, was an excellent way to make sure Rebekah had made her choice by free-will. I certainly can't know what they were thinking, but I know Laban's future tactics. I base a lot of my distrust of Laban on the reaction of Eliezer. He was ready to leave, and he was God's man. There was, however, a good result from this request.

The family had agreed the night before that Rebekah should go. But what are her thoughts? As we watch, we may be struggling with what she should do. What are a few more days out of a lifetime? It sounds like a good thing. At this point in the story, with limited information, I think she should have stayed. I understand what God was doing, but let her mom have a day or two. However, I have seen in future Scriptures the dangers of delay with this family. I know better. This is an encrypted hint. Only God knows all the story; look to see what He is doing first and foremost.

Nahor's family may have had respect for God, but they were nowhere on the same page as Abraham. He believed God; he walked with God. The best I can tell, Nahor's family only knew that there was a God that Abraham believed and trusted. They saw the blessing Abraham had experienced. Abraham's God had to be real. But in idol worship, the method of worship was manipulation.

Abraham's God was always doing something. God's works were visible, and He cannot be manipulated. For this family to manipulate the situation, it would take time. But Rebekah was leaving. Was Laban's solution to stall the departure and see what more you could obtain from wealthy Abraham?

I see some good advice here for those who have family from either side that does not believe or trust in God. The family is important. If I am right about Bethuel and his family, and history proves my suspicions, God did allow Bethuel to have a "say" about his daughter's marriage – but that is all. If you remember he didn't see anything good or bad about it, so he approved – because he had to. The advice is to keep God in the process.

Marriage is an institution created by God that is needed to produce family and ongoing joy. It is also used by those who don't believe in God. Faithfulness is not part of Satan's plan, but man created in the image and likeness of God desires faithfulness. The need for marriage is in our DNA. Satan's plan is to do anything to destroy what he can about marriage as God had designed. Satan has developed many alternate and substitute ways. These have an edge of oppression and are about "taking," not "giving." They fail at some point—the need for faithfulness and trust will not be found outside of God's plan.

Rebekah's belief that God was forming her marriage was right. Isaac would prove to be a very faithful husband, not perfect but faithful. He is one of the few men in the Old Testament's stories who didn't fall prey to the "multiple-wife lie." Rebekah was to be his one and only, just as God designed.

So, what is my point about unsaved family members? Simply, when they live by emotions and physical motivation, any advice given is at best, questionable.

We must love and respect our parents. But at some point, when seeking God's direction, we must first follow God. If He is involved, it should be evident to all.

Concerns from others are to be addressed. When God is involved the correct answer will be easy to see.

You and the one who is to be your spiritual soul-mate for life must slowly work through any issues. Seek good spiritual leaders who talk and think Bible; pray and ask for understanding from God. If you can prove all things using God's ways, those questioning the union should default to leaving the choice up to you. Remember these are things done before the engagement. If one or both seeking to get married are not born-again believers, marriage is not your problem. Your relationship with God should already be established – and not just so you can get married.

Did the mother and brother want Rebekah to stay because they would miss her, or was it just buying time until they could benefit from Abraham's wealth and wishes? I think the test was given by God's Spirit. When God has been at work, you will know it.

Rebekah's Choice

Gen 24:58 *And they called Rebekah, and said unto her, Wilt thou go with this man? And she said I will go.*

We now have a marriage proposal and an official acceptance. Rebekah has agreed to go with this man so that she can marry Isaac. "I will go" will soon become "I do." Our culture struggles with this kind of marriage set up. The press would insert questions here like, what if she doesn't like him, or what if he is ugly or obnoxious. They would reject him because he didn't come riding in on his white stallion to romance Rebekah. "Where is the romance?" they would cry. (Hang on, it's in the story - you will see.) Real romance is not something you watch it is something you live. It may start with dating, but it is the years of faithful love in marriage that produce a romance the movies cannot film.

The media would utterly reject the concept of a marriage not built upon physical appearance and mushy romantic moments. Stop and think about this. They are trying to get you to buy their products. They promote the physical and emotional because that is what they can manipulate. The most effective part of movies and television is visual communication—a physical thing. Yes, they add music and dialog for emotional manipulation, but most of their power is in the ability to control the imagination of the people watching visually. The amount of time spent on wardrobe and makeup is staggering. What we see is nowhere near real. Then they utilize great lighting techniques and choose their camera angles very carefully. Super attractive people are not found, they are made – "made over" that is. Then the advertising world picks up where the movies leave off and define what beauty is, what happiness is, what romance is, and what love is. And somehow it is connected to the product they want you to buy. God doesn't want you to buy His product; it is free. He created it all for us. What God wants is for us to be part of His Kingdom, starting now.

The media tries to create romantic moments. They add tears, shyness, starry-eyed music, awkward dialogue and throw in some obstacles to stop the romance from developing. Their method is to create a story meant to pull at your heartstrings. Massive efforts of manipulation keep you watching and spending your money. They know what they are doing. Romance is a big deal for the media. It is because we are wired for romance. But permanent romance is found in a godly marriage. Real romance can last a lifetime when done God's way.

Physical appearance is one of those things that can be manipulated easily. A person like Rebekah, who has a servant's heart, or Isaac, who spent his life providing for his family, has nothing to offer the physically-based media world. This world teaches us to marry based on appearance, talent, money, or possessions. The cool, tough looking guy finds a mutual attraction with the perfect and gorgeous leading lady. The ability to provide and maintain all that is necessary to create a family is not part of the fantasy romance ways of the media. If you will notice, prince charming almost always seems to be well-financed. The "happily- ever-after music" is added to the ending. It's not that way in real life. But the media world is not concerned with your marital success. They seem to benefit from broken marriages and lonely people. Not only do they neglect integrity, but they also preach against and laugh at anything connected to God.

In the real story, Rebekah exercised her free-will. She understood what God was doing. She would miss her family, but God had called her to go, and she was ready. It may seem impossible for her to prepare to go so quickly, but she didn't need to take much of anything. Abraham and Isaac were ready to receive her and provide everything she needed.

It is part of the all-encompassing story of the Church. When the Bride of Christ is snatched away, she will take nothing because everything she is leaving behind is not necessary for the Covenant Agreement. Jesus has prepared a place already. Think back a few verses. Eliezer gave Rebekah gifts of raiment or clothing. My guess is they were pure white.

I will never get over how God can tell two stories at the same time – Isaac and Rebekah and Jesus and His Bride the Church. I understand God's approach to dating and marriage will not be readily received in our culture. There could be "push-back" from family, friends, and society in general. Nevertheless, God's way is not man's ways. My personal experience followed the path that I am showing you here. The fundamental concept of a spiritual connection followed by a year of engagement for emotional bonding produced a fifty-year marriage. We did not know what we were doing, but God did. Like Daniel, we purposed in our hearts to do it God's way the best we could, and God blessed.

Having read the stories found later in the Bible about Laban, I am surprised that the next verse was written. How God can shut down the mouth of those who want the ways of the world is beyond my comprehension – but he did. Laban stood by speechless. And notice, his father has been entirely written out of the story. When you say, "Yes, I will go" to Jesus, you have changed families.

There is no reason given to those of us who are examining this story as to why Bethuel has left the story. But Rebekah had just married into the family of God. The same thing that happens to us at the time of salvation. Satan has acted as the father of the fallen world since the fall in the Garden. But it is about time, as it was with Rebekah's father Bethuel, for Satan to be written out of the story.

Permission Granted

Gen 24:59 *And they sent away Rebekah their sister, and her nurse, and Abraham's servant, and his men.*

So, we now have permission for Eliezer to leave and for his men to head back home with the bride for Isaac. We also see something new, Rebekah's nurse is also going, perhaps as part of Rebekah's dowry.

A dowry of property, gifts or money is a transfer from the parents at the marriage of a daughter. It is their contribution to start the new family. A Dowry contrasts with the concept of the payment by the groom or his family to the bride's parents called the "bride-price." Abraham had made sure that he more than compensated for their loss of Rebekah's hands to help in day to day life. The family needed to respond to tradition with a dowry. Wealth given from the bride's family to the groom or his family was not needed in this marriage.

However, there was something they could do to help Rebekah in the transition. The most significant gift they could have given Rebekah was the nurse that had been with her from childhood. We will see in verse 24:61 there were other young unmarried girls, damsels that accompanied Rebekah on the journey back to Isaac. I see the picture of the Church as we leave this earth - we will not be going alone. Those near to us will be making the journey with us. What better gift to take to the Marriage Supper of the Lamb but our close friends and family?

We will now hear an amazing speech from Rebekah's family. I have not developed the story of Nahor's family much, but it is evident they had some connection to idolatry, at least as the years went by. Knowing that Rebekah's family had some respect for God didn't rule out that they were also romancing false idols.

Faithfulness is not an option in a relationship. Worshiping do-nothing-gods clouds the truth of who is in control and opens the door to deception. Want a good example? Look at the result of marriage the Boomer Generation's way. The idol of pride and lust and thinking that "we" know better than God has almost destroyed the concept of family in this country. But it doesn't have to. God is still the only one in control. It is still a free choice whom you worship.

Blessing Given

Gen 24:60 *And they blessed Rebekah, and said unto her, Thou art our sister, be thou the mother of thousands of millions, and let thy seed possess the gate of those which hate them.*

Rebekah's family knew about God from Abraham. They had heard the incredible stories of their great uncle. The ten camel caravan and the expensive gifts proved what they had heard. God's Spirit was heavy upon all the proceedings, and they spoke what they knew and offered it as a blessing to Rebekah.

These few words fit perfectly with what God told Abraham years ago. I fear they knew about God more than they knew God. Their respect for what God was doing speaks volumes. Many people in our culture ride and stay on the edges near the Church. They often use the same words as believers, and they approve of what the Church is doing. But they may never make that necessary step from knowledge to a belief based on trust. It is like dating without commitment.

The family has responded to God's plan. Their desires agree with God's eternal ideas. They understood the Covenant Relationship that Abraham had with God enough to know that Rebekah was going to be the mother of thousands of millions. They also believed that God was going to bless her and her new husband against the enemies of God. They recognized that Isaac's family would sit at the Gate. In other words, rule over those that hate them because of their faith in God.

She Arose

Gen 24:61 *And Rebekah arose, and her damsels and they rode upon the camels and followed the man: and the servant took Rebekah, and went his way.*

With these words, Rebekah was ready to leave. What we have seen is spiritual maturity ruling over emotion, and it all happened in less than twenty-four hours of time. Have you noticed the storyteller often took giant steps in time without telling us? We move several hundred miles and many weeks from verse ten to eleven - not uncommon in the art of storytelling. God does it better than anyone. The storyteller leaves out unnecessary parts to move the story to the conclusion. We are about to do that again as we move to verse 62.

Some commentators believe that there might be more time in verse 54: *And they did eat and drink, he and the men that were with him, and tarried all night; and they rose up in the morning, and he said, Send me away unto my master.*

They suggest additional days went by. While that is possible in storytelling, it doesn't read that way. It is best to think that God did the preparations, and she was ready to go the next morning. It also fits with the snatching away of the Bride of Christ. It will happen without warning, and there will be no earthly delay.

This rapid decision should not be used by anyone to rush through the normal dating-engagement-marriage process. You may be tired of hearing it, but you must prove all things in the dating stage – even if it takes time. Physical and emotional desires are very impatient, and they do not want to wait for anything. But the pain and suffering of failure in a marriage are all around us. Use wisdom, test out what your soul-mate and your heart are doing. Next, to your eternal salvation, a lifelong commitment will be the most critical decision you will ever make. Don't mess it up with Hollywood and society's false teachings. You have everything to lose, and they have everything to gain.

So, what if you did not get married this way with God's involvement? In my life's story, I saw the involvement of God and thank Him for the lifetime of marital happiness and contentment. Because of "The Lie" many marriages today are falling apart. You may think your marriage was a mistake because you did not seek God during the process. This could be wrong thinking. How can this book help you?

If you go back and think about all that has happened, you may find that God was involved, but you just did not realize it. Read and apply Isaac and Rebekah's story. Jesus said in Mark 10:9 ...*therefore God hath joined together, let not man put asunder.*

I hope you got the, "what God joined together" part.

Divorce happens, but how often is it just people taking apart what God put together. Marriage is a real-life situation that God has given us so we can understand His love. Without marriage and family, humanity might never see what true love looks like.

Understanding God's plan of marriage can and has restored many marriages. Although it may not be easy, it will be worth it. A difficult marriage situation may be what is needed to open eyes to what God has for you.

We are getting close to showing the "right word" that is so often used at the wrong time. It is the "power-word" of "The Lie." But first, let's look at Isaac. He is the other part of this story, and we have not seen him at all.

Isaac's story

Gen 24:62 *And Isaac came from the way of the well Lahai-roi; for he dwelt in the south country.*

Back home, weeks away, Isaac has been waiting. We can safely believe he knew what his father was doing, but information traveled slowly in those days. Nobody posted pictures of Rebekah on Facebook ruining the surprise for Isaac. He was just busy doing the work needed to maintain life. He and his father no longer lived in the same place. Abraham was some distance away. After his wife Sarah died, some time went by and Abraham would remarry. That story is in Genesis Chapter Twenty-five. But Abraham was passing the blessing of the Covenant Relationship forward to his son Isaac. Life would go on for everybody, but God is telling the next step in the story of the Covenant Relationship. Abraham slowly left the narrative, and the bloodline and blessing moved to Isaac.

We find Isaac in a similar place to where we found Rebekah. Isaac is at a very special well. It is named Beer-lahai-roi. It is a living spring between the wilderness Kadesh and Bered in the south country. It is believed to have been named by Hagar because she heard God speak there. God provided the water she and her son needed to stay alive – most scholars seem to think this is the same well where we first see Isaac in this story. The story is found in Genesis 21:17-19.

Here is how it goes: Sarah could not have children, so she gave Hagar, her handmaid, to Abraham to father a child. Not a good move. Sarah was interfering with what God was doing. It is from this relationship that Ishmael was born, a child and future people group that often interfered with the Covenant family throughout the Old Testament. As with all the stories in the Bible, when somebody takes an alternate approach to God's plans for marriage, things don't turn out so great. Just like today, the baggage from an improper sexual relationship will stay with you forever - a good reason to take your time and see what God is going to provide for you.

Most likely this was the "well" that saved Ishmael after his mother heard the voice of the Angel of God. These many years later, Isaac had moved there and started his farming operations. It seemed he took over the head of the family position because he is now called "master" by Eliezer, and he had his mother's tent. It seems that Abraham had passed the Covenant Blessing and all that goes with it to Isaac. What Isaac needed was his

Bride to continue the chosen family.

It doesn't appear it was clear to Abraham what the chosen family was to do. His family knew they would bless all nations, but as you read the Old Testament, it seems they seldom got it right. Nobody truly understood what God was doing until after the Resurrection of Jesus. At that point, for the first time, everything made sense.

Did you catch the hint above? You will never understand everything God is doing. But you will be able to see that He is involved in your life. Trust Him – you will be blessed.

Seventeen

Isaac Was Doing As He Should – He Was In the Field

The place we should be.

Gen 24:63-65 *And Isaac went out to meditate in the field at the eventide: and he lifted up his eyes, and saw, and, behold, the camels were coming.*

And Rebekah lifted up her eyes, and when she saw Isaac, she lighted off the camel

For she had said unto the servant, What man is this that walketh in the field to meet us? And the servant had said, It is my master: therefore she took a vail, and covered herself.

So, what had Isaac been doing? He had been meditating in the field. In our picture of Jesus and His Bride, we have heard Jesus talk about His fields, ... I say unto you, Lift up your eyes, and look on the fields; for they are white already to harvest (John 4:35). If I had to guess, Isaac was in the field thinking about his new job as the patriarch of the family. He knew he must have children to carry on the Covenant Agreement with God. Was he praying for Eliezer's success? I think that would be a good guess.

Gen 24:63 *And Isaac went out to meditate in the field at the eventide: and he lifted up his eyes, and saw, and, behold, the camels were coming.*

During the dating process, prayer will keep you focused on what God is doing. Isaac was a true believer; he did not interfere with God's plan for his marriage. Isaac is one of the few Old Testament Patriarchs who did not change God's ways of marriage. Rebekah was his one and only, and Isaac was doing what he should have been doing when he looked up and saw the caravan coming. He was in the fields, a place to provide for his family.

At her first sight of him, Rebekah saw Isaac doing what she hoped he would be doing. You can almost hear their hearts skip a beat even today, thousands of years later. Do you hear the music of anticipation?

Years ago, when I saw for the first time the one I might marry, there were no camels or fields. It was a college class welcome party for the incoming freshmen held on the church parking lot. I knew who she was, but suddenly I realized she might be the one.

I was not ready for this, and that was true. It took months for me to ask her out, and six months of dating to prove all things, including my new revelation that I was ready to be married.

Isaac was already past the "I want to be married" stage. He had things prepared, and he saw the caravan coming. He knew by the appearance of the camels they were his and could see there were more people than was sent out by his father. Did he see the one in white? I know it doesn't tell us that she was dressed in white in the Bible. But the church will be in white when Jesus receives his bride, so indulge me – she was dressed in white in my mind's eye. You will have to put up with my imagination.

She saw him.

Gen 24:64 *And Rebekah lifted up her eyes, and when she saw Isaac, she lighted off the camel.*

She knew he was the one the first time she saw him because he was where he was supposed to be. This reminds me of my story. Being where you should be is one of those subtle messages you can use to defeat "The Lie." Both Rebekah and Isaac were where they should have been—doing the work of the Lord. I am not talking about preaching, or Bible-teaching, singing, attending church, but merely taking care of the family. That is our job, the work that God has given us. Inside that job, we live out our relationship with our Savior.

It is because of our relationship with Jesus that we do the preaching, teaching, singing, attending church, and ministering to others. One of the significant influences of my young life was when my father spent many hours in what I now call practical discipleship. He and my mother always had an "adopted family" who were attending Bible College. Dad didn't disciple them in Bible studies but applied God's way of kingdom life by serving and helping them find God's answers to everyday problems. He did this by meeting needs they could not accomplish - things like fixing a broken car, an open door for a meal, or maybe a listening ear in a time of need. You serve God while you live your life and provide for your family. I just wrote something important again; you may want to underline this and draw an arrow to it.

Your first job is your family – do it right, and you will be blessed. Let your family see God through you in your everyday living. Watching my parents do this made an impact on me as well as those they helped.

How did Rebekah know that this one man in a field might be her new husband? Good question. The answer is it's a spiritual thing. Today, God moves through His indwelling Spirit, and sometimes you just know things like this. I can't explain it, but somehow you know for sure. It's discernment from God. When Rebekah looked up, she knew and immediately acted.

Getting off a camel is not an easy thing, but it must have been for Rebekah. My wife thinks Rebekah was in great physical shape from running up and down the steps of the well. She tells me that Rebekah could have somersaulted off that camel.

The text says she "lighted off." I loved it that the KJV used this old and unusual terminology. I had to stop and see what

God is saying by looking up these words in the old Strong's Dictionary. He could have said she got off the camel; I would have understood and moved on. But that is not what God wrote here. I can't pass this up, what is hiding in these words?

Most translations say, dismounted, quickly dismounted, got down, jumped down (I like this one) and one said alighted. Okay, how tedious – it means Rebekah got down. But the Hebrew word carries some passion.

Naphal (naw-fal'); a primitive root; **to fall**, in a great variety of applications (intransitive or causative, literal or figurative).

This definition looks like algebra to me, but those two words from the primitive root means "to fall." I told you there was romance in this story. Hollywood eat your heart out. Hollywood knows nothing about romance, compared to this. Rebekah saw the man of her dreams, and she got off the camel to meet him. Did Rebekah fall off in her haste? Was she "falling for Isaac"?

Wikipedia says, "The metaphor (of falling for someone) appears to emphasize that the process is in some way uncontrollable and risky." I guess this means as in an accident. There is a risky feeling if it is a one-sided deal. Would the "falling" be reciprocated?

But we know this first meeting was not an accident. We have seen God at work. And we witnessed that both Isaac and Rebekah relinquished control of their lives and let God arrange their marriage. There was no risky feeling here.

Yea, you got it. Rebekah fell for Isaac.

There was indeed a risk as I stood there that Saturday at the college function and thought about how this girl, now my wife of so many years, could be overwhelming for me to get to know.

Marriage involved great responsibility. Could I take on the responsibility of a husband which I knew marriage required? Was I ready? The responsibilities of a husband are listed at the end of this story.

It is fair to say, marriage was not quite yet in my "bucket list" vocabulary, but I did know you marry people you date. What if I was wrong?

I didn't know about proving all things, but my shyness served me well as we moved slowly getting to know each other in a church setting, little by little. It took months before I asked her out on a college group activity. You may ask, when did I fall off my camel? After several months of dating, it became evident. We were never apart, and we both knew we never wanted to be apart. My wife is one of four daughters. So, her dad would be getting a son. While dating, I was always there. They knew, and my folks knew before I knew. I had fallen off my camel.

Gen 24:65 *For she had said unto the servant, What man is this that walketh in the field to meet us? And the servant had said, It is my master: therefore she took a veil, and covered herself.*

Rebekah maintained proper behavior always. Notice that the first thing she did was start to prove all things. She asked, "Is this the man that God has chosen for me?" That is my translation anyway. She asked this before falling off the camel.

I know what most of you are thinking. What happened to the romance in all this? Did you miss it? It says she took a veil and covered herself. Vail (or veil) means to cover. I use the old spelling because this is an old story. Marriage, by God's design, is a process of discovery. Where is the romance? It's hidden behind the veil. Rebekah understood this, but we have lost all understanding of real romance in our culture. Let me explain.

Eighteen

Where Is The Romance?

Gen 24:66 *And the servant told Isaac all things that he had done.*

From a little research, it appears that the veil has a long history. From what I can find, the oldest record of a wedding veil is in this story. Was it already a custom in that part of the world? I will give you my best guess; the oldest reliable history we have is Biblical. Could this story be the first time it happened?

Was Rebekah naturally just adding to the mystery of romance? Most of the things we do in our modern day "romance-style" weddings are somehow associated with Jewish wedding customs. These things were just being placed into existence with the call of Abraham and our story about Rebekah and Isaac. They have become our traditions. Some of them may have started with Rebekah and Isaac.

The marriage ceremony tells an unbelievable story, particularly the Hebrew wedding. The old Hebrew practice started with the snatching of the bride, and all the details in the old Jewish wedding traditions tell the story of Jesus and His Bride. Jewish weddings model the story of Jesus. Ultimately, I believe the practices introduced were from God. God loves to tell the Story about His Son Jesus and has embedded it all over the Bible. In the Bible, it is His-Story – Jesus' story is the only history we need for eternal life.

There are many tales as to why the veil came into being, most of them stemmed from the Greek and Roman periods, centuries after our story here. But I think there is a practical side we can use to see something about marriage.

What I am about to say stands in complete opposition to our culture. A non-believer may not understand.

Marriage is a mystery as Paul wrote in Ephesians 5:32. It is all connected to Jesus and His Bride. But I think the concept of mystery is also very simple and natural. God has chosen to reveal Himself to those who want Him. It is not a sudden, full revelation; it is a process of desire and time. The more we read the Bible God has given us, the more we know. It takes a relationship, and God has provided full revelation, but we must grow in our understanding slowly. The more we know about God, the more we love our Creator. The romance is in the discovery process. Rebekah's veil started the romance – and there is no indication that the romance ever ended for Isaac.

We say that marriage pictures the relationship of Jesus and His Bride – but I think the relationship of Jesus and His Bride pictures what marriage should be like. I think Paul agrees. We've got it backward.

It took many years of marriage to comprehend this. Starting with dating I began to understand my wife, and it was good. Years later you would think I would have it all down, but no. She still surprises me on many occasions. She knows more about me, and I about her than anybody else, but we still do not know everything. It is the mystery and the unexpected things that make a marriage alive. We are still exploring the world we live in. It is the mystery and the unexpected moments that are cherished. But our culture still tries to steal the mystery with "The Lie."

As I have already said, sexual things are not part of this story. That is because sexual things are part of the mystery. It is a gift from God to each couple who chooses a covenant marriage. When two people decide to spend their lives as one, there is absolutely no need for anybody else. They are satisfied physically, emotionally, and spiritually.

In our media-driven culture, the mysteries of marriage can be seen anytime and on any level. Here is the problem. The secrets of the discovery of the physical and emotional parts of soul-mates keep being stolen and replaced with mental images of lust. What God gave as a gift is now corrupted to the point that the mystery is lost forever. Instead of finding God's answer to physical satisfaction, Satan and his World System have used photography to create lust and oppressive thoughts. The idea, "you can do better" replaces the oneness found in a marriage of faith and trust.

Pornography

These false images of lust are everywhere. Everybody knows that pornography is causing significant issues with marriages. It is an addiction that controls every aspect of a person's life. The longer one is involved, the more difficult the escape. Get help. Can it be defeated - yes, but only with the help of God's Spirit, His Written Word, and in most cases with the help of another true believer as an accountability partner. There are several things that have proven very successful in escaping the trap.

Pornography is a topic beyond what we can cover, but if you have an addiction to porn, finding and keeping your soul-mate will require a detox from this "lie." Detox is possible if the addiction is replaced with the truth. A person must resolve this issue to experience life as God has planned and let the Spirit of God slowly remove those false images that Satan has placed in your head.

But the real issue I fear is the "G" rated "porn" we ignore. The minds of our culture do not even notice the suggestive words and wardrobes. What a few years ago was called pornography is now everywhere all the time and seen as normal.

My point with all this is that God has given us a gift, and we need to protect our children and ourselves. It starts with computer blocks and unreachable cloud-based accountability systems.

The truth must be discussed and made plain to see. I will leave this discussion to others with more experience on how to handle the addiction to pornography.

Kissing

Kissing is part of romance, right? It is in there, but you need to refocus your concept of romance to God's thoughts. Yes, God has a concept of romance; it's in the Bible. And God has things to say about kissing. One of the biggest questions that come up in a biblical study of marriage is, "What about the first kiss." "Kissing" is missing in Rebekah's story, but not in the Bible. Here is a quick review of some principles on kissing.

Kissing is an expected part of dating in our culture; pre-teens are waiting for their first kiss. Is that okay? That is up to you to decide. But the first kiss can be part of "The Lie." See what you think. It is part of proving all things.

> Proverbs 27:6 *Faithful are the wounds of a friend, but the* **kisses** *of an enemy are deceitful.*

Defraud is a synonym for deceiving.

- Defraud means to take away from, deceit, trickery, or cheating – it means intentional deception.

- Honesty cannot be compartmentalized. When someone is willing to cheat in one area, you can expect deception in another.

- Notice "kissing" is in this verse (Proverbs 27:6).

- Kissing is seen in the Bible as "good" and "bad."

- Kissing can lead you to believe one thing but result in another.

Matt 26:47-48 And while he yet spake, lo, Judas, one of the twelve, came, and with him a great multitude with swords and staves, from the chief priests and elders of the people. Now he that betrayed him gave them a sign, saying, Whomsoever I shall kiss, that same is he: hold him fast. And forthwith he came to Jesus, and said, Hail, master; and kissed him.

Kissing provides us with another subtle message for those involved in finding a soul-mate. Kissing can be a form of deception leading to private agendas. It's a caution sign to the wise on kissing. When a person smells food, the body reacts naturally with a desire to eat. The physical contact of kissing starts another natural reaction. This innate desire can cause "self" desire to take over. A person who would never dream of defrauding finds "animal like" instinct in control. The wise will take heed of this warning. Many a kiss has led to fraud and ended a ministry.

Few would consider kissing an issue. What is in an innocent kiss? I think it depends on a lot of things. Remember when you are looking for a soul-mate, just be the person you want to find. Go only places, dress, and act like you would want to see in your future mate. Like that old saying: "You can't change the bait after you catch the fish." If you find yourself in the wrong place with the wrong person, what is intended as an innocent kiss can send some very wrong messages. Please take note; I am only discussing how to prove all things. And kissing is an easy way to defraud.

The servant told Isaac all.

Gen 24:66 And the servant told Isaac all things that he had done.

As in the beginning, the storyteller leaves out the major trip back from Mesopotamia. I am sure there were stories to tell. But God, as the Master Storyteller, has an objective, and we are ready to see the conclusion and learn what we need to know. I have found many commentary writers who say that Rebekah arrived, and the story moved to the tent.

I object to this view – that is movie thinking.

We need to see some possible things that took place between the words in the story. Notice that Eliezer told Isaac ALL the things that he had done. That is more than a short conversation in a field. Isaac was a man of great character, and I think an appropriate amount of time was given for Rebekah and her damsels to adjust. That time would also allow Eliezer time to tell Isaac all he needed to know thoroughly. It is here that the engagement period starts. How much time between here and the end of the story cannot be determined from the text, but I suspect the correct answer would be as long as it took for the couple to work through some simple steps of engagement. They needed to bond together correctly. It is possible the story rapidly moved to the physical stage of marriage. But Abraham and Isaac were God's men on earth, and we would expect them not to rush anything significant.

I know there are cases where dating, and engagement happens in a flash. I know a couple, a little older than me, that met while young and were married very quickly. They have remained happily married for at least sixty years plus. But I also know that many marriages struggle, and all too often fail because they did not prove all things. If God is in control, the process of dating and marriage may not take long. For the story of Isaac and Rebekah, proving God's involvement had already been accomplished. So, in this "arranged marriage," the engagement period could have been short. Everybody knew God was in control.

We do know that Isaac needed to hear the story about the camels, brother, and mother with all the details – and he did. God's involvement was monumental for the one who was to carry the Covenant of his father Abraham forward. No mistake could be allowed. A man of integrity will take the time and spend the effort to verify everything. The stories told by Eliezer would be accepted because Isaac trusted this servant.

Leaving and Cleaving

I'm just guessing, but Isaac would not move forward until it was proper. Here are the kinds of things that take place during the engagement period. Many of these things were already in place for this couple, but not everything.

The purpose of engagement is what you would expect to happen. It is where two begin bonding together emotionally, thinking alike, spending time with each other, learning how to walk together.

Engagement is also the beginning of the process of leaving the father and mother to cleave unto each other. This leaving will also include other family members and friends in which you hold emotional bonds. For example, there will be much you will never tell your best friend and anything you would tell your best friend you would also say to your spouse. The close ties of the past will become less critical compared to the oneness you are creating with your life-long mate. The couple begins to work together as a team – "I" and "me" become "we."

There are practical issues that need to be worked out such as planning a wedding together – It's not just her job. There are bigger things to plan together like the house, car, and jobs. Even planning the honeymoon should be done together. And the financial budget is a major together necessity. In other words, engagement is learning to work together for the good of both and the marriage; Phil 2: 3-4.

The amount of time from Isaac and Rebekah's first sight of each other is not essential for us to know. I just wanted to insert the possibility that there was some time spent in the final preparations. The amount of time needed for people in our culture to move through this process will vary. Rushing through the steps may not allow the emotional glue to set and form a lifelong bond. The two getting married should be so concerned about the other that each can have self-control for the sake of the other.

Nineteen

We Are Ready to Expose "The Lie."

Gen 24:67 *And Isaac brought her into his mother Sarah's tent and took Rebekah, and she became his wife, and he loved her: and Isaac was comforted after his mother's death.*

It sounds like she got off the camel and they moved to the tent, and she became his wife. Stop and think about this. They had been on camels for weeks, and men of integrity like Isaac and the unnamed servant always consider the needs of others. As with the long trips, the text leaves out a lot of details.

Rebekah and her damsels needed time to adjust to their new home. So, to me, this reads that Isaac moved them into his mother's tent, which was now Rebekah's home as Isaac's wife. Then when everyone was rested and ready, they moved forward with the ceremony and the physical part of marriage.

There is a word that has been missing in this story. Nowhere have we seen this word that our culture used so freely. It has not once appeared in the text. It is the "right word" our culture continuously seems to use at the wrong time, as I mentioned in the introduction. The word we always expected to see now appears. **Love.**

"He loved her."

(You may want to dog-ear this page so you can find it again.)
The word "love" seems to be all-inclusive; she was perfect. But
don't you find it strange that in this sixty-seven-verse story, one
of the longest in the Bible, the term "love" doesn't appear until
almost the last word. And this is a story about marriage. Our
culture would be in an uproar if they noticed this. They would
say, "That is not how it works."

Love is part of the dating process - right? NO!!

In the introduction, I hinted that failure in dating and
marriage is a result of how we use the "right" word at the wrong
time. The right word is "love." In Rebekah's and Isaac's story
the word "love" appears at the end of the marriage process.

In our culture, we are taught love is found at the beginning
of the dating process. The idea is we date and fall in love. But
what we see in this story is we are to prove all things, then love
appears. After you prove all things, you make an agreement to
marry and bond two souls together. Then comes marriage and
the word "love" becomes real. The entire process is the process
of falling in love.

Don't Miss This

If you start the process by thinking you are in love, it might be an
infatuation or lust. You cannot love what you do not know, and
you can't know something until you prove all things. Rebekah
saw many things she needed to see. Things like integrity, respect,
kindness, going the extra mile, honesty, trustworthiness, and a
desire for God. And the final proof is a commitment to marry
for life. Love grows strong under the trust that was built during
the entire process.

How does this compare to the time you said "yes" to Jesus?
"Lord, I accept your offer of Salvation." For some people, it can
take extra time to understand who Jesus is and what He is doing.

Most who accepted Christ as their Savior do so for a reason, and I suspect it wasn't because they had fallen in love.

There are lots of reasons to accept Jesus' offer of salvation. They find it as a path to eternal life or a way to escape hell, here on earth or at judgment time. Both are valid and prevalent reasons. Perhaps the decision is made because of a need for a trustworthy friend, someone to help you through life. The key thoughts are faith and trust. I think you will agree, whatever level of love you had for Jesus the day you were born-again, that love has grown greater every year. The same is true for a biblically based marriage. Love is the result of the marriage.

Did you notice that the story doesn't tell us that Rebekah loved Isaac? I think Rebekah already loved Isaac because of what God had done. She already knew about Isaac from the events back home and the stories Eliezer must have told her. We don't know what Rebekah's life was like back home, but it is probably a "given" that she had desired for a husband who would love her. She found her salvation for life here on earth with Isaac. A man who would provide, protect, and give her children. She loved Isaac because she had already decided in her heart; she could trust him to be her husband.

The word "love" did not enter the story as our culture would mandate, believing it all starts with some kind of "magical thing" called love. You can't love someone until you know them. Love, as God designed is more than a passing emotion. Love is a result of a commitment and years of bonding together. At some point, the one you love is just as important as you are to yourself. Trust becomes oneness, and that is pure love.

So, what is "The Lie, this great deception?"

It is simple. In our culture, "The Lie" is the use of the word "love" for what is really "lust." Lust only brings disappointment, one of Satan's favorite tools.

You know what I mean. The movies depict how they think it

works. "I love you - will you marry me?" as a first reaction may not be the best start. A lasting marriage should be the result of a God-designed process starting with dating where you test all things.

All the pre-preparation of proving "all things" and those hours of emotional bonding during engagement leads to a marriage where love grows.

That is the way Salvation works with Jesus - we grow in our relationship. The more you know, the more you love. Marriage glues two people together into "one" when the process is done God's way.

Following God's way results in lasting romantic love. As the years go by, your desire is so intertwined with your soul-mate's wishes you can't tell your desires from his/her desires. If your soul-mate is not happy, neither are you and you look for ways to fix things. If pain is experienced, you suffer also. God's plan for marriage produces a marriage that cannot be broken apart.

"The Lie" is based on a simple and straightforward concept: life is only about the physical. In the background is hidden the core idea there is no God. The concept of marriage is wrongly-based on random luck. You stumble onto somebody that might do, and that's all you got.

In our story, Rebekah became Isaac's wife, and he loved her. Again, notice the catchphrase, "loved" is at the end of the process, not the start. True biblical love comes after God's plan is carried out.

While arranged marriages are not the way it is done today, we can still maintain all the above in the process of finding a mate. God, family, and biblical principles are to be in place. One does not just fall in true love by sight as Hollywood suggests. Sight may provide the attraction but proving all things with a covenant agreement is the foundation needed for a lasting marriage.

A marriage can be messed up by improper dating. If couples know how their mates behaved outside of God's "rules" before marriage, it can create a lack of trust later in the marriage. They know what their mate is capable of doing. God has a plan for marriage, so His ways need to be included in dating.

If your marriage is a mess, it is still possible to go back and find or restore God in your relationship. You cannot start over, but you can still prove all things. I didn't say it would be easy, but those married can still go through the process of proving all things even if they started out not including God in their relationship. Sometimes God will use marriage to help you understand your relationship with Him. God was involved in your marriage process even if you did not know it. Reaffirm a commitment and build trust in your relationship based on God's Word.

In cases of physical abuse and drug-related nightmares, seek out professional advice. Most pastors know of qualified professional Christian counselors God has trained to help.

Too many people jump out of a marriage just like they jumped into it. Before bridges are burned, think about a biblical solution – keep God in this process.

An essential component for restoration is prayer on everybody's part – you, your spouse, your pastor, your friends, and your qualified Christian counselor. God can reveal an answer, and this answer should become obvious to all.

What makes a marriage great?

Jesus often taught in parables, stories that demonstrated the truth. They were nothing more than delightful tales for those who did not understand or want to know. But Jesus' stories are full of truth to those who were seeking it.

Matthew recorded several parables about seeds – the ones planted to grow wheat. The good seeds represented God's truth, and the bad seeds represented Satan's lies in Matthew 13:34-35. I remind you of this because many of the stories presented in the Bible also have this characteristic. Some are historical and happened in real life, others are parables, but inside the action are hidden pictures of the Kingdom of God to come. A great example is our narrative of Isaac and Rebekah. It is not a parable; it occurred. But like a parable, it carries a parallel message of Jesus and the Church.

Why does God have so much to say about marriage? Because marriage gives a perfect representation of Jesus and His Bride in the eternal kingdom to come. It's a great mystery – but only to those who do not study God's Word. It's a beautiful picture, and God doesn't want anyone messing with His "art."

Ephesian 5:22-32 talks about a great mystery. Paul is speaking concerning Christ and the church. This passage is often used to help define the roles of husband and wife. However, Paul is pointing out the focus is in verse 32: but I speak concerning Christ and the church. This shows that the natural understanding of the relationship between husband and wife was to be used to illustrate a more challenging relationship between Christ and His Church. Satan has destroyed the real definition of marriage, so the picture we are left with is dim at best. Look for it; the great mystery can still be seen. We just need to clear up the definition of God's plan for marriage, so the picture can be seen clearly again, stomping out what Satan has made it.

Reject "The Lie" and find lasting romance and love as God designed us to have.

Twenty

The Biblical Responsibilities of a Husband

Here is the list, I referred to earlier, of the Biblical Responsibilities in a marriage. These are things that must be thought about before you start dating because you marry people you date.

The first responsibility is to love her. Eph 5:25 - *Husbands, love your wives, even as Christ also loved the church, and gave himself for it.*

"As" is the keyword here. It places on the table unconditional and sacrificial love. Christ is our example because He loves us even with all our faults. Love is a key point - we are not worthy of His love and struggle to understand it. If you look at mankind, why should Jesus love us - we are not that lovable. But He does. It is inside God's plan for the family that we can see what unconditional and sacrificial love is like. I think his plan for marriage, children, and grandchildren help us understand the concept of love. Husbands are to love their wife unconditionally.

The second responsibility is to dwell with her. 1 Pet 3:7 - *Likewise, ye husbands, dwell with them according to knowledge, giving honor unto the wife, as unto the weaker vessel, and as being heirs together of the grace of life; that your prayers be not hindered.*

It's "being there" for each other. This dwelling is more than roommates sharing the expense. It's best friends in love spiritually, emotionally and physically. Companions who are living all that life has to offer and living it together. Dwelling produces a sense of completeness and comfort. There is no hint of loneliness. When you are together with your soul-mate, it is the only time of real rest. It's not just in the same house together. Dwelling with her includes the children knowing that Dad wants to spend time with Mom. The love relationship is felt by all in the family. Remember, this responsibility comes with "teeth"-failure here is a hindrance to prayer as it says in 1 Pet 3:7.

The third responsibility is to know her. It is also found in 1 Pet 3:7 above. To dwell, you must know her. Know her likes and dislikes, her best and worst memories and the things that bring her joy and peace. Dwelling is all about spending time together that you do have. When you do, you will know your soul-mate.

The Fourth responsibility is to honor her, still found in 1 Pet 3:7. She needs to know the respect you have for her, that she is a rare jewel. Respect for her is to be shown to others by your actions and the way you talk about her. (Calling her the "old lady" is disrespectful – it is not funny to her; it is an embarrassment.) By being in control of yourself - not loud, angry, or with excessive actions at home or before others. A man's behavior must be as a gentleman to all women, but the honor given his wife should stand out. And this honor and respect must not be just public. It must be continuous - especially in the home.

The Fifth responsibility is to provide for her, found in 1 Tim 5:8-*But if any provide not for his own, and especially for those of his own house, he hath denied the faith, and is worse than an infidel.*

Paul has told us that the husband is to accept the role of leadership in the home in Eph 5:23, so "his" here is referring to the husband.

This may not be received well in our culture. It may be totally rejected by a growing segment of our society that a man must be the one who provides. Just because our culture doesn't like these ideas, doesn't change the fact that they are from God.

A man must be willing to accept the responsibility of providing for his wife and family. This doesn't mean he is the only one providing.

As I said in the generational divide chapter, the new normal has not worked out well. The current default normal has not "proved" itself as a satisfying way to produce a balanced and successful family.

It is true, a woman is not at the mercy of a male-dominated society, as history has generally recorded. That form of oppression has changed in some ways. But God's plan for the family has not changed. God's design was for family. And a family must have a committed provider. These responsibilities have biblical roots and a long history of success.

There is plenty of flexibility in how a family works; my point is God's design is for a man to willingly place his wife and family as a top priority. Read this and all the other responsibilities as a willingness and a commitment to each other in marriage. This list is not a daily guide to who does what. Oneness in marriage seeks the best answers to all situations. It may mean the husband waits for his new Xbox in order to buy the new washing machine. Family needs come first.

This responsibility to provide means more than just the basics: food, shelter, and clothing – it means to provide for "all" needs. It should include a feeling of security. Secure from physical danger; of needing basics, and security that you will always be there. This may include, if possible, life insurance, disability insurance or a plan to care for the family if the man cannot do so in the future as seen with Jesus in John 19:26-27.

And of course, the man must fill the position of father to the children. This must include providing spiritually by keeping the family in church.

The sixth responsibility is to teach her, found in 1 Cor 14:35. - *And if they will learn anything, let them ask their husbands at home: for it is a shame for women to speak in the church.*

In context, this is referring to speaking in "tongues" or other languages. In application, it says that the man is to be the spiritual leader. But in many cases, the man is missing from Bible study, prayer and church life. He must be seeking spiritual growth to fulfill this responsibility.

The "anything" part of this verse might mean he is to teach her what her father neglected: to change a tire, to live on a budget, to balance a checkbook, to mow the yard, and other things that go with providing for the family in case the husband is not there.

The seventh responsibility is to protect her. Eph 5:23 - *For the husband is the head of the wife, even as Christ is the head of the church: and he is the savior of the body.*

See also Proverbs 18:10 and Matt 12:29. To protect goes beyond security. It means providing a feeling of protection, with things like a car that is not prone to break down in the middle of nowhere.

It would extend to protecting her from people who want to use her for their own glory or to control her actions to justify their own. Guard against those who say you must: breastfeed, cannot work outside of the home, or maybe say you must homeschool, cook from scratch or other personal choices. People often want you to do what they do to justify their choice. Shield her from this abuse and make your own decision on all these issues prayerfully.

The man is to protect his family from the pressures of the world and dealing with the wrong people. Protection is always needed. Think about Genesis chapter 3 and the need for Adam to step up and defend against the snake.

Proverbs 18:10- *The name of the LORD is a strong tower: the righteous runneth into it and is safe.* A husband is to provide that "SAFE" place for his wife. Matt 12:29- *Or else how can one enter into a strong man's house, and spoil his goods, except he first bind the strong man? and then he will spoil his house.* We are to be the strong man for our wife. By strong, I emphasize "spiritual strength."

The eighth responsibility is to be her husband and only her husband. This **should be the** easiest, but to some, unfortunately, it may not be.

From 1 Timothy Chapter Three, we see that God has character qualities for a man in leadership, and all men who are in a position of leadership if they are married. *"To be a husband of one wife,"* means to be a good husband. To be a faithful husband: This could mean more than you think.

Faithful Husbands:

- Must be committed with the mind (Gen 6:5, 8:21, Jeremiah 17:9, Matt 15:19.) Where are his thoughts taking him?

- Must be committed with the eyes (Job 31:1.) What are his eyes seeing? This includes pornography - which can kill a marriage.

- Must be committed with the lips. Watch joking and flirting. What is this saying to others?

- Must be committed with the hands. Watch hugging. What is the reason for the hug?

- Must be committed with the feet. (I Cor 6:18 flee immorality.) Where are you going and why are you going there?

These are all issues of trust. To put it bluntly, "If you are "shopping," you can't be trusted." How do you rate as a faithful husband?

To be a faithful father is a list for another time, but I think you are getting the idea.

Twenty One

Biblical Submission to Each Other

B efore we move to the biblical responsibilities of a wife, we need to include one important common element. I have always found the biblical responsibilities for the wives more difficult to compile. As a Bible teacher, I tend to focus on the men's list. Submission is the first item on her list and is more difficult to teach because I am a male, and this responsibility is an encompassing concept for both husband and wife. After the Baby Boomer rebellion, our culture has been taught to hate the word: submission. Submission is part of oneness - it is part of marriage. The common misunderstanding is part of the deceptive lie that has taken over.

Before we look at her list, we must stop and connect this back to the men's list. Paul tells us in Eph 5:21 that husbands and wives are to be "Submitting yourselves one to another in fear of God." Submission is for both. I see submission in all eight of the items in the men's list, but the concept must be amplified. Culture gets in the way of what God teaches, and words and definitions get all twisted around.

Here is the point: Couples that marry God's way become intertwined and live as "one," and submission to each other becomes automatic. They don't need this point of submission amplified because co-submission is how they live. But then again, that is far from true in the current Satan inspired World System.

We need to supplement this and make a big deal about it.

When biblical marriage was removed from our culture back in the sixties, God's equality and submission went out the window. Yes, I know there are single-parent households where the topic of submission seems to be a moot point. One parent can raise children, but it can come at a cost. Part of the price is the loss of understanding by children in how submission in marriage works. When children have never seen it modeled, they may find it hard to do. It may not become automatic when they marry. What is the answer to this dilemma? "Keep your kids in Church" and personally teach and show them the need to read the Bible. This can help replace what the World System has taken from us.

I find it interesting that the younger generations have developed a powerful desire to maintain a two-parent family. They are even trying to return to marriage as their anchor. This is true for some non-believers who are doing it without the Truth from the Spirit of God to help. Time will tell if they can make it work. It is not hard to understand why they want this since God created us with a DNA that needs family even without His Spirit. Submission is the way to success with God's plan. In the Book of Joshua, there is a story about 2 ½ tribes that failed to submit to God's plan for them to dwell with Him in the Promised Land. They asked to live on the other side of the river, and it all sounded good. God never commented on their action. God blessed them and gave them riches beyond what they asked. The story is in Joshua 22:6-8. But the result of their non-submission to God's plan eventually became early failure and destruction. As they experienced Satan's attack, they were the first to be carried off by their enemies.

Submission is the standard way of life (Eph 5:22–6:9) for every Spirit-filled Christian. We are to be humble and submissive to each other. No believer is inherently superior to any other believer. In our standing before God, we are equal in every way (Gal 3:28). We should also see the command is unqualified and applies to every Christian. God's plan has no allowance for things like abilities, education, knowledge of Scripture, spiritual maturity, or anything else. Submission is to be a way of life.

People that detest the concept of submission forget it is 100% both ways. It's all part of the problem we face as a result of the fall. When you remove the spirit of truth, you don't have much left.

Men were born with the need to protect, and women were born to need protection. Predators seem to always focus first on women and children. God creates with wisdom, and a man is also to submit to his wife. To lead, he must have the right answers, and often "her" point of view may be the key to him making the right decision. Her viewpoint is needed to help protect his leadership position. Think of it as co-submission.

The Biblical Responsibilities of a Wife.

The first responsibility is to be under submission, found in Eph 5:22 –*Wives, submit yourselves unto your own husbands, as unto the Lord.*

This role of submission God gave to a wife is not a less prominent role, only different. Oneness makes submitting easy to understand. She submits to her husband's leadership as he submits to God's leadership.

Ask a quarterback how vital the roles of the other players are to the game of football. His leadership role may seem to get more glory, but he is also the one with the most exposure and risk of failure. Remember, in football the objective is winning the game. In marriage, it's accomplishing the mission God has given his creation.

Submission cannot be demanded, only given freely. "Your own husbands" defines her submission to the one man God has given her and creates a balance that he is hers as a personal, intimate possession (Song 2:16; 6:3; 7:10). She submits to the man she possesses as her own. This oneness is the same "as to the Lord." Submission is an act of obedience to the Lord who has given this command regardless of her husband's worthiness or spiritual condition. God's way establishes a strong "oneness" that cannot be broken.

Non-submission to each other in marriage is like wearing a sign that says, "We will not obey God." Here is that pitfall again: non-submission can be transferred to children. The result is disobedience and falling away of children from family and God. Many problems with children result from issues between parents and their relationship with each other.

The second responsibility is to love him, as seen in Titus 2:4 – *That they may teach the young women to be sober, to love their husbands, to love their children.*

Know how your husband "feels" loved. Know his "love language:" touch, words, time, gifts, or care. To love is shown by being a testimony that your husband is your best friend.

With age, part of the responsibility of a wife is to teach younger women how to love their husbands. This is to help combat Satan's attack on the family and the Great Mystery. Each person trying to figure it out on his own takes too much time out of a short life.

The third responsibility is to reverence him – in Eph 5:2 *For the husband is the head of the wife, even as Christ is the head of the church: and he is the savior of the body.*

The proper attitude should picture and demonstrate respect for him. Remember the husband (as a father) is a picture of Christ to the children. The relationship between husband and wife in the area of respect will be an influence on a child's attitude toward God. Men, it is your job to be like Christ to your wife.

A wife should speak highly of her husband – not criticizing him in public – even when he is wrong. If problems exist, they should be worked out in private. A little study of reverence can be found in Lev 19-30, 2 Sam 9:6, 1 Kings 1:31, Est 3:2,5, Ps 89:7, Matt 21:37, Luke 20:13, Heb 12:9,28. It's a great mystery.

The fourth responsibility is to be his "help-meet" – Gen 2:18 – *And the LORD God said, It is not good that the man should be alone; I will make him an help meet for him.*

The concept here is for the wife to help her husband with the mission. I once read a missionary wife's testimony that explains this very well. She said:

I know the day I was called to the mission field. I know the very hour and minute.

The very spot I was standing.

The people who were around me. I even have pictures to show.

It was the day I said, "I do."

God did not give Adam a personal slave. He gave him someone to complete the ministry team. The wife's assignment is to help her husband with the special abilities God has given her.

The fifth responsibility is to be his representative, found in Eph 5:27 – *That he might present it to himself a glorious church, not have spot, or wrinkle, or any such thing; but that it should be holy and without blemish.*

There are many things that happen every day in which the wife must assume the leadership role when "Dad" is away. The Husband cannot be two places at once. God's design of oneness where the husband and wife function as one makes these times easy. When both think alike the decisions made are the same even if one is not present.

As the Church is the representative of Christ, the wife is the representative of the husband. The actions, appearance, conversation, faithfulness - everything done reflects on her marriage and her relationship with Christ.

The sixth responsibility is found in both lists: to provide for him – Titus 2:4 *That they may teach the young women to be sober, to love their husbands, to love their children, To be discreet, chaste, keepers at home, good, obedient to their own husbands, that the word of God be not blasphemed.*

"Keepers at home" means to provide more than just the basics: food, shelter, and clothing – it means "all" of his needs. He needs to feel wanted. He needs to know she wants him to perform his eight responsibilities. He must know she cares about his day at work. It would include the feeling of security and that she is always there for him and the children. She is a good mother.

He needs her to be his closest friend—the one he turns to in times of difficulty. She can't be totally consumed by the kids, her job, the house or herself. He may seem okay, but that is part of his responsibility to be the strong one. Sometimes he may not be okay. Oneness of the relationship should include warning signs. He may not tell her, but she should be able to discern when he is going through tough times and needs a shoulder to lean on.

The seventh responsibility is to protect Him. Proverbs 7:7:4-5 - *Say unto wisdom, Thou art my sister; and call understanding thy kinswoman: That they may keep thee from the strange woman, from the stranger which flattereth with her words.*

This may seem like an unusual point, but a wife needs to understand that she can protect her husband from the "strange woman." This is wisdom. I have used the verse a little out of context, but it does apply. Every wife should know that her husband is being hunted by the "strange woman with wanton eyes" (Isaiah 3:16-24). Protect him outside the house at work, and inside the house from the screen. Even commercials are aimed at men. She may not see it, but he will struggle to ignore it in this culture. We all should be careful with what we watch. A fall starts with the eyes. In Genesis chapter three we see that Eve saw, wanted, and took. First Corinthians chapter seven tells us how to avoid physical and mental fornication. She should protect her husband and be all he ever needs.

As it was for him, there is an eighth responsibility for her. To be his wife and only his wife – I find it sad, but in today's culture we must add this to "her" List.

Faithful Wives:

- Must be committed with the mind. Where are her thoughts taking her?

- Must be committed with the eyes. What are her eyes seeing?

- Must be committed with the lips. Watch joking, and flirting. What is she saying to others?

- Must be committed with the hands. Watch hugging. What is the reason for the hug?

- Must be committed with the feet, flee immorality (1st Cor 6:18.) Where is she going?

To be a faithful mother is a list for another time, but I think you are getting the idea.

Conclusion: Christ and the Church show the proper pattern for dating, engagement, and marriage. Men and women are different by God's design, and when God's plan for dating and engagement are used to join two spirits and two souls, the physical marriage is very natural and a blessing to all involved. Let the romance begin.

Satan's plan from the very beginning was to destroy or at least blur the picture. The Word of God is one of those things that Satan cannot change; the picture is still there for us to follow. For those who choose God's "ways," there will be the blessing of finding "heaven on this earth," as near as we will ever come until Christ Himself returns to rule.

Twenty Two

Finding God's Balance in Marriage

There are two extremes often found in marriages which cause failure to accomplish what God designed marriage to do. The first extreme is ignoring your spouse's needs. That often results in divorce or the "roommate" relationship – living together but not as one.

The second is becoming "too married" and ignoring what God put us here to do. The focus is so much on your own life that you leave God out. The "love relationship" with each other must be in balance with a mutual love for God. Being too married leaves everybody else out, sometimes this may even include children.

Finding a balance between the two extremes is found in the Lordship of Christ as seen in Eph 5:22-33. A marriage is only as healthy as the couple's relationship with God. Oh, I think I just wrote something important! The essence of Lordship and knowing God is seen in Job 22:21, Ps 9:10 and 1 Cor 2:8-9. It seems the closer one comes to God the more sinful one feels. Subsequently, God's love is felt in a deeper way, and we start to understand our value in the kingdom. Practical Lordship is walking with God as in Phil 1:27, Phil 3:20, Eph 4:1.

As for the story of Rebekah and Isaac, we have looked at all sixty-seven verses. But this story is played out every day. For those who have stuck with me, you must decide what to do with it. I have related the history of marriage as far as I can to God's point of view. If you turn on the TV, go to a movie, read a questionable romance novel or get on the Internet, you will see most scripts have been swung as far away from God as possible. Satan's plan is to use emotions and the physical as the primary focus of dating, the first stage of marriage. He wants to keep God out of the picture. When God is left out, a relationship may seem perfectly fine, but as the unexpected pressures of life build, failure is often the result.

Trying to add God back into marriage when he has been left out of the planning stages might be difficult. But it can be done start with prayer. Learning what marriage means to God will change hearts and help detox from "The Lie."

Caution! No matter how hard one tries, emotions will begin to affect thinking. If single, consider some form of group dating. It not only offers a "checks and balances" system but makes breaking up much less painful. A rule to live by: Spend as much time getting spiritually ready for a date as you do to get ready physically. Remember God defined marriage as a bonding and covenant between two people that links one soul to another soul for a lifetime.

God gave us a free choice. As for me, I want to be married God's way.

There are several concepts I did not cover here, but are in the Appendix, plus a "list" or two on dating you may like – or hate. It's up to you.

Your goal is to glorify God. There is no better way than using His definition of marriage in obedience to please Him. Not only can you please God, but the security and joy of loving your soul-mate never results in second-place ribbons.

Watching grandchildren grow in their understanding and faith in God is very satisfying. It sure beats the "haven't seen or heard from my children in years" comments that are so common in today's culture. Loneliness is Satan's plan. A lasting, loving, and productive family is God's plan.

If you choose the path of biblical dating, it might take more time to discern whom you should date. Do not fall into a "poor me" syndrome. Instead, flip "The Lie." Reject the thought that dating is only for fun. Believe the truth that dating is for proving all things and that you marry people you date. Look at it as a real-life treasure hunt. Like Eliezer, plan an adventure to see what God will do. Join a caravan, go find a place of pure, clean, living water and look for somebody serving God because they want Him. Your Rebekah or Isaac is there at the well, go find each other.

Footnote: This book is perfect for those who are starting the Dating process. It also has topics that parents with children need to teach. For those who have not had a good experience with dating or marriage, the principles still work. It may require adjusting in the way you think and how you approach this beautiful thing called marriage.

Appendix A

Preparing For A Date

I considered including this in Isaac's and Rebekah's story, but since dating is not in the Bible, the word or the concept, it was placed here for easy comprehension. This is a checklist of questions and thoughts to determine readiness to date.

If you fail in one of the points, you are not ready.

Events leading up to date

Start by pondering these questions:

Are you ready? And by this, I mean spiritually.

- Are they ready? Have you seen a spiritual side to the person you are considering to date?

- Remember: Standards need to be high – But you must be realistic. We are all working to be like Christ.

- If not ready, then identify areas of needed improvement and ask the Lord to strengthen you with biblical truth. In other words, fix it with the Word of God.

Look up these verses and meditate on them. Col 3:15-16 and Phil 2:10-11.

Here may be the "Key" to success: Look at the way the decision to date was made. Can you show events that God used to bring you together for this date? Things like "I was at the mall, and he/she looked at me" doesn't count. When God is not in this process, wait. See if you can discover how God is bringing you together. Time spent here is a good investment. Remember: You marry people you date.

CAUTION: Don't let "self" convince you of something that is not true.

It is usually best if the man initiates the date. God's plan is for the man to be the spiritual leader. If the leadership role is reversed from the very beginning, God's plan for marriage may get off on the wrong foot. Look at Adam and Eve and the role reversal results.

But what if the guy is too shy? That is more than possible. The ability of some men to lead has been damaged by our changing culture. My suggestion is to try a small group situation that could eliminate awkwardness. Become acquainted with each other first. God can overcome any kind of issue. In a group, your brothers and sisters in Christ can help mend the damage done by our society to both men and women.

Events during a date

Plan out the specific events of a date, having the approval of parents - if applicable. The following is out of context, but it still applies. Jeremiah 29:11 – *For I know the thoughts that I think toward you, saith the LORD, thoughts of peace, and not of evil, to give you an expected end.*

It's simple; God has plan for us, with an expected end. We should model our lives, including dating, with a plan. A plan would include an expected end to the date. During the date, stick totheplan. Ps 119:112 *I have inclined mine heart to perform thy statutes always, even unto the end.* Again, this verse is not talking about dating, but the concept is applicable. Don't miss this: planning and sticking to the plan avoids the appearance of evil. By sticking to an approved plan, you can guarantee blamelessness.

Involve others on a date. If a problem comes up, like a flat tire, it won't alter the plan if you are in a group. Blamelessness is easier if you avoid being alone together. The choice of the group you chose is critical. Remember, group dating keeps everyone accountable. In a group of God-fearing people "self," will most likely maintain control and keep all actions pure.

What do I mean by group dating? A group date is a time spent getting to know each other without a commitment to an implied relationship. You have time and opportunities to prove that there is a spiritual attraction — time to see if God is in the process. Church activities, small groups, going out to get ice cream any kind of situation that does not automatically label the activity as a commitment. Avoiding the cultural "image" of being a couple removes the pain of breaking up. If the spiritual attraction is present, things to do to be together will become obvious to both.

Keep it non-physical. Remember Rebekah's purity was stated in two ways to make sure all understood she was blameless. It was in our story in Genesis 24:16. We find in 1st Cor 7:1-2 *Now concerning the things of which ye wrote unto me: It is good for a man not to touch a woman.* And in 2 Cor 11:2 *For I am jealous over you with godly jealousy: for I have espoused you to one husband, that I may present you as a chaste virgin to Christ.*

Ruth 2:8-9 says: *have I not charged the young men that they should not touch thee?* Boaz wanted his future wife protected in purity, even before he knew she would be his wife. The picture here is Christ and his bride to be. We, the bride of Christ, must maintain this purity. The Holy Spirit dwells in us. I may be reaching here, but picture the Ark of the Covenant. The only way it could be touched (moved) was through a ring.

God gave the gift of sex to those that marry. Taking this

outside of marriage, even talking or joking, weakens what God has planned for his creation. Hollywood has all but destroyed what God intends for those married. Protect your purity. God's way is the only way.

How far is too far? Use the father/mother rule. Guys treat your date like you would treat your mother/sister. Gals treat your date like you would treat your father/brother. Holding hands, kissing, hugging takes on the proper perspective here.

By dating God's way, you will find that engagement, marriage, and family relationships function correctly. Problems that turn up later in marriage can be linked to improper dating. It cannot be said too many times; God's way is the only way.

What to do after the first date

It is easy, try to state the spiritual attraction. If, while proving all things, you did not discern where God was part of their life, slow down and ask why. When the spiritual attraction is perceived, the natural attraction can slowly over time move forward. You will not have to struggle and wonder. Proving all things generates romance.

If you have read this story, notice the kind of things that Rebekah and Isaac discovered about each other. That's what you should be expecting to see in your experience. It is hard to miss all my hints, and hopefully, you picked up on the ways to prove all things.

When somebody is only looking to have "fun" by dating, then temporary fun may conceal the truth needed to achieve a lifelong romance. A little time spent getting to know the real person before you start dating is a small price to pay for a lifetime of joy.

The deception, "The Lie," is when we reject God's ways, we ultimately reject God. If you are expecting me to detail how to date you may have missed the point. If God is part of the process, it will all happen very spiritually, and it will be obvious to all who are watching.

Appendix B

Alternate Substitutes for Marriage

What do I mean by an alternate marriage relationship? It is simple. Any relationship that is not in God's plan, as He intended, is an alternate marriage relationship. And they all fall short of what God wants us to have.

I have used the terms married, spouse, couple, and soulmate, throughout this book to identify a man and woman who married using God's plan in Genesis 2:24. Many words today have been changed to be gender neutral, but we will use God's definitions.

It is not my purpose to discuss all the substitute ideas for God's plan for marriage. He created marriage so "man" would not be alone, as He stated in Genesis 2:18. His solution eliminates that lonely feeling so common today. It sounds like the issue of "loneliness" is a result of rejecting God's solution – biblical marriage.

There is not enough space in this book to detail the vast variations that have been substituted for God's plan for marriage. God's design results in oneness and co-submission which produces family and a lifetime of growth and excitement. The romance built into God's plan endures for a lifetime.

As we saw detailed in the story of Isaac and Rebekah, the key lies in the oneness and co-submission produced by proper dating and proving all things. God's provision in marriage avoids the loneliness element and removes the concept of oppression and domination from the relationship.

Some of the alternate marriage concepts may provide some form of relationship, but hiding in the background is a huge potential for manipulation and victimization of the innocent with oppressive domination. If nothing else, these replacements for biblical marriage deny the privilege of having a son or daughter in the image of the couple. Denying this God-given right is a form of oppression.

Marriage God's way is free of such things; it results in the submission of two people into oneness and reproduces itself in the form of children. It is a relationship based on the fullness of life as intended by our Creator. Any relationship that denies another to live as created by God is oppressive.

Holding and watching your child grow up, seeing yourself and your soul-mate in that child creates a family unit and longevity that alternate lifestyles have no possible way to produce. Biblical marriage is a lifelong affair that is resistive to seduction and interference from outside influences and possible predators. It seems alternative marriage styles must use aggressive recruiting because they cannot reproduce on their own. Because they can't have natural children, they must depend on recruitment. They must sell their alternate idea that there is another way.

I used the term "oppression" and "predator" from the Bible's lead in Genesis chapter 19 where we see both. These negative assessments are now removed from our cultural view. All we see now is that the alternative marriage arrangements are suggested as an acceptable option to God's plan for marriage. History through the centuries is ignored and lost in the modern conversation.

But this perspective is very new to society. Our market-driven culture has slowly redefined thinking with alternate and unproven answers to God's plan for marriage. Lust does not provide a lifetime solution to loneliness – only God can provide that answer.

It is true that marriage from the start has never been "picture perfect." The Bible is full of bad examples for us to consider, exposing misuses such as simultaneous multiple-wife marriages, adultery, and an almost endless list of abusive sexual encounters. However, marriage as an institution still survives and remains fundamentally unchanged for those who do it God's way.

God's design for marriage is the way society was designed to work. At the core of our social order was a family structured around marriage. And it has functioned brilliantly.

Look back to recent history.

As we have seen, marriage, God's way, made us strong until the Baby Boomers redefined it. Before the nineteen-sixty social revolution, a man or a woman who lived together outside of marriage raised a lot of eyebrows. The majority said it was wrong. After a few decades of ignoring marriage, a "living together" relationship lost any shock value. It seems as marriage became optional, evil imaginations have jumped in to fill the gap with alternate arrangements. Society is ripe for these substitute concepts. When you have lost the answer, you seek a solution. Nevertheless, the answer that actually works is the one we found in Genesis 24.

Have you noticed, those who advocate these alternate marriage concepts seem to thrive on controversy? With more controversy comes more media time. And this means more political strength is obtained. It is the same technique used by the Boomers to change the concept of marriage during their social revolution on injustice based on skin color. The enormous political power given to them by the media allowed them to change anything they desired – and it is the same technique being used today. The boomer's desire started as a fight against the oppression of skin color, fueled by silence from the Church, and resulted in the rejection of God's plan for marriage. The current sexual revolution just seems to be seeking power.

The Boomers didn't think about what was going to happen around the edges of their rebellion. The thought of family was never in the mix. They were looking for social justice for all people – which is the American way and a God thing. With their new power, they began to find freedom from authority, so they could "fix" society. And it is here that things went too far.

With God removed from their life, they could do as they pleased, it is the natural result of rejecting God. The "free-love" movement was little more than a fringe undertaking, but with the introduction of the birth control pill, the need for marriage was destroyed. If you were "cool" you didn't give legal marriage a second thought. Looking back at the Boomer's rebellion, we now see it has not worked. Many from my generation have returned to their roots and formed marriages, but not before changing and producing a society with a skewed view of marriage.

The Cost

Born-again Boomers now know the cost of not having a biblical marriage. Children and grandchildren are affected. The alternate lifestyles of today create even more baggage and pain for these future generations.

The final flaw in alternate marriages is longevity. Biblical marriage, as designed by God, was to grow together creating "oneness" that changes with age. A biblical marriage produces a relationship where your soul-mate is the only person you ever need. Oneness matures over time. You age together and meet the ever-changing needs of your spouse. The biblical marriage produces a core satisfaction. The end product of God's plan for marriage is a self-growing and ever enlarging family. Loneliness was never part of God's plan. Something that substitute relationships cannot provide.

Rejecting God's plan for marriage leads to rejecting God's Word, which leads to rejecting God Himself. This removes the joy and hope we have in God's plan of salvation. The is no hope without Eternity with our Creator. If you take God out of His Creation, expect failure.

Appendix C

What is Meant by, "Born Again?" "Saved?"

If you have read this far in my book, I assume you are a seeker of God. Some non believers may question the value of my writing and ask if it is worth their time. However, my hope is that you are interested in seeking God's ways and following Him.

What do I mean by the term, "born-again?" The wording comes from the mouth of Jesus. He was talking to a Jewish religious leader who was struggling with who Jesus was.

> *Jesus answered and said unto him, Verily, verily, I say unto thee, Except a man be **born again**, he cannot see the kingdom of God.*
> John 3:3

Jesus explained it all in the discussion that followed. Born-again means born again spiritually. Back in Gen 2:16-17 God told the first man created that he would die if he ate of the forbidden tree. Everybody knows the story. Adam and his wife Eve rejected God by disobeying God's commandment, and they died that very day spiritually as seen in Genesis chapter 3. But they lived physically for many years and had children, who were born spiritually dead, like their father Adam.

Spiritual death means they lost their connection to God. And without God, they had no hope of eternal life. God had foreseen this possibility and had a restoration plan. God cannot lie, so death was the mandated price for sin.

However, God would accept a substitute death in their place. In other words, an innocent man could pay the price for the sin by dying in their place. God would accept the substitute payment, and they could live. There was no innocent man, so God sent His only Son to pay the price by dying on the Cross.

The process is called being born-again or being "saved."

Perhaps you have never made a decision about God; it is simple. God wants us and has given His Son to die and pay the price of sin for all who will believe. It starts by asking forgiveness for sin and deciding to follow Jesus. All men live in fear of death, but this is not a devastating issue for those who choose the path of Jesus for their lives. It is not always easy, but it comes with a perfect rest from fear. Life can be full of twists and turns but being born-again and knowing about Eternity in Heaven with Jesus overpowers all evil or hardships thrown at us.

There is no magical collection of words that you need to know, just a heart desire for God. Here are a few short Bible passages to help. I used Romans because all the critical doctrine about salvation is near each other and easy to understand.

It starts by seeing that nothing you can do is enough to get you to Heaven. You cannot do it by yourself.

For all have sinned, and come short of the glory of God;
    Romans 3:23

Salvation is not a new thing, "It is written" of old. It was always God's plan because all people need help - they cannot pay the price for their sin – that would take an innocent person and there are none.

As it is written, There is none righteous, no, not one:
    Romans 3:10

The problem is universal, like with the blind man Jesus healed, all humans are born blind to the spiritual truth of God.

God's plan was to have a relationship with His Creation. It was men who rejected God. A Holy God cannot have a relationship with sin.

> *Wherefore, as by man sin entered into the world, and death by sin; and so death passed upon all men, for that all have sinned:*
> Romans 5:12

Sin is a big deal, and the price of sin has always been death. Sin will not be part of God's Eternal Kingdom. However, God's amazing love and grace provide a way back to Him by removing our sin.

> *For the wages of sin is death, but the gift of God is eternal life through Jesus Christ our Lord.*
> Romans 6:23

What is God's way for fallen man?

> *But God commendeth his love toward us, in that, while we were yet sinners, Christ died for us.*
> Romans 5:8

How can you be saved - born again into the family of God? It is in this next passage - confess and believe.

> *That if thou shalt confess with thy mouth the Lord Jesus, and shalt believe in thine heart that God hath raised him from the dead, thou shalt be saved. For with the heart man believeth unto righteousness, and with the mouth confession is made unto salvation.*
> Romans 10:9-10

Who can do this? The answer is anybody. Remember, that God will hear. Jesus reached out to blind men, an adulterous woman, and even the self-righteous Pharisees. It was their choice to say "yes" or "no."

For whosoever shall call upon the name of the Lord shall be saved.
Romans 10:13

No one is excluded from God's plan of Salvation. All men and women are the same to God. Salvation is humbling. Salvation is by faith – you just trust the truth God has spoken and written. Man cannot change the fact that God still saves.

So then faith cometh by hearing and hearing by the word of God.
Romans 10:17

Yes, it is all written in the Bible. We should be so thankful that not only did God say it, He had it written down and preserved so all can understand. God's truth will never change. God was saying, "I Love you so much" when He paid the price for our sins. Jesus made it possible for those who want Him to live eternally with Him in the Kingdom forever.

In your own way and words ask forgiveness for your sins. Thank Jesus for dying to pay for your sins. Tell Him you accept Him to be Lord of your life and that you want to live for Him. This is your "rebirth" into the family of God. This is your "salvation" through Jesus Christ.

Then next, get to know Jesus better. Some start at the beginning with the first Book of the Bible called Genesis, but my suggestion is the book of Mark. This is where Jesus came to earth to walk with men for three years.

Then perhaps go to the rest of the Gospels; Matthew, Luke, and John. I would also read 1st John and then go to Genesis.

No matter where you start, just start.

I suggest setting up a few minutes a day and read all the Bible from cover to cover. It takes less than 80 hours, and that is about 15 minutes a day for a year to read all the Bible. Few ever do this. That's less time a day than the commercials during one regular TV show. Look for Jesus everywhere you read. The more you look, the more you will find Him. The Bible tells the story of Jesus and God's plan to restore the Kingdom. You may be stunned to see how much stuff you think you know that is actually not in the Bible.

And there is one more essential thing. If you do not have a church home, find one. This is a critical step for growth. Look for a church that teaches "the Bible," not "books" about the Bible. Books about the Bible have their place, but the only truly reliable source of truth is the Word of God itself - preserved throughout the ages.

Seek friends who enjoy serving the Lord and are also spending time in God's Book. They can help you grow quickly. It is called discipleship. They are easy to find; they never quit talking about Jesus and the Bible. You will usually see them helping other people in every way possible. My guess is they will find you.

What is Discipleship?

Discipleship is based on the word "disciple." In Bible terms, a disciple means a "learner." However, discipleship is not just a Bible expression. You can see hands-on discipleship everywhere you go. The trainee at the fast food restaurant is being "discipled" in the art of taking fast food orders.

The most famous disciples were the Twelve Disciples of Jesus. They were taught the art of spiritual living as God had designed and they ministered the truth about what Jesus accomplished on the Cross. Modern-day discipleship is teaching somebody else what you know about Jesus and the Bible. If you know anything, you know more than most people in the world.

Many Churches have an organized discipleship ministry. They have identified and trained experienced believers to help develop and grow newer believers. The process facilitates rapid growth in a person's weak spiritual areas. The result is years of progress taking place in a few months of time.

I highly recommend one-on-one discipleship, particularly if you are a new believer. If your church doesn't have an organized ministry, look around and find a spirit filled person. If you ask them to discuss a topic in the Bible, you will find them willing and able to teach you many things.

If your concern is marriage, find a couple that is obviously centered on God and seek some of their secrets. Don't expect to find perfection, but if you listen closely, you will hear that somewhere God was involved in their dating-marriage relationship. Find those who are successful and see how they did it. And when it comes to marriage, the most successful will be those who did marriage God's way.

Remaining Single

Not all people will marry. The Apostle Paul is an example of somebody who had the God-given gift to remain single. When you are willing to follow Christ wherever he takes you, it may mean you will remain single, but you will not be alone. This does not mean that you "will" remain single, only that you are willing. This shows your true heart. Are you willing to follow God over "self?"

Singles can reproduce spiritually. Ministry can, in some ways, be easier if you have the gift to remain single. You will not have to balance your time with your husband/wife. There is nothing wrong with being single. God gives this gift as Paul wrote in 1st Corinthians.

> 1 Cor 7:7-9 *For I would that all men were even as I myself. But every man hath his proper gift of God, one after this manner, and another after that. I say therefore to the unmarried and widows; It is good for them if they abide even as I. But if they cannot contain, let them marry: for it is better to marry than to burn.*

The key to understanding is in verse nine. If you have the gift to remain single, then you will not struggle with that fact. If you struggle, then it would be best if you seek your soul-mate and serve God together.

More Scripture to search

- John 10:10 – Source of more than we need.
- Col 2:10 – Made complete.
- Ps 23:1 – You shall not want.
- 1 Cor 3:7 – You can't do it.
- 1 Sam 16:7 - Don't focus on the outside.

Here is a quick test to help you determine the path you should take. Your answers tell the condition of "self" and will help you make a spiritual decision instead of an emotional choice.

- Can Jesus lead you?
- How do you obey Jesus?
- Do you desire to read the Bible?
- Do you pray because you see the value or only when trouble comes?
- How do you love the brethren?

  John 13:35 *Of **this** shall all men know that ye are my disciples if ye have love one to another.*

Do you have a burden for the lost of this world?

The answers to these questions are spiritual answers. They demonstrate your relationship with Jesus. But there is also an emotional and physical answer. How do you know if you can remain single serving God? I cannot answer that question. Nevertheless, I have known people who have been given this gift to remain single. Somehow, they have perfect peace serving the Lord Jesus Christ and have no need for a soul-mate. If God gives you that gift, you will know.

Being single is not for most people, but those that seek this path will find their satisfaction with life in ministering the Gospel and serving others. Like Paul said, *For I would that all men were even as I myself.*

The Trilogy of God's Plan for Marriage

This book is part of a series showing God's truth as found in Old Manuscripts – specifically the Bible. The first one is called *The Dating Story* showing the procedure of correct biblical dating. The story is found hidden in Genesis chapter 24. What we see is how God is involved in the marriage process of Isaac and Rebekah. It should be the same for all of us.

The second is called *The Family Story*, and here we find how God's covenant love works within "family," as seen inside the story of Ruth.

The Marriage Story, found in Song of Songs, is the third book showing the results you might expect from living God's plan for marriage. It is perhaps different than you think.

Each of these books stand alone, but starting with God as part of the dating experience helps us to live what we will see in this Song of Songs. Understanding covenant love helps strengthen the family experience. The result is we sing our own Song of Songs.